AWAKEN THE CHILD IN YOU

notionpress.com

AWAKEN THE CHILD IN YOU

GUNJAN SAHAY

notionpress.com

Notion Press

Old No. 38, New No. 6,

McNichols Road, Chetpet,

Chennai - 600 031

First Published by Notion Press 2015

ISBN: 978-93-5206-360-4

PREFACE

There is a child within every man and woman. But in today's world, what we call the 'rat race' has sent the child into near permanent slumber. As a result, survival at any cost has come to take precedence over the enjoyment of life, and we've lost touch with our capacity to enjoy life, to take pleasure in the very act of living.

"Awaken the Child in You" is an attempt to chart a path toward joy and success by connecting with the child within, and awakening it. It explains how the child within each one of us is silenced and locked away as we grow up, and offers insights on how to once again awaken it as we journey through life.

A key insight that I explore and develop in the following pages is that people who are genuinely happy with their lives have their inner child awake and kicking in their hearts.

The child within gives a different outlook to life — an outlook that is usually missing from life for most of us, and without which neither a free mind nor a free heart is possible.

At every stage in life — when we are in school, when we are employed, when we are setting up our own business venture or taking the family business to the next level, when we embark on married life, when we have kids, and when we finally settle down under the fading twilight of old age—ensuring that the inner child is awake will make our earthly sojourn more meaningful as well as memorable.

What I have penned down in this book is easier said than done. But then, are we not social animals, the ones higher up the evolutionary chart, the ones who have the power to change the world more than any other being–given that we are the ones who have the heart and courage to not only face tough situations but to emerge victorious from them?

This book might not offer a concrete solution for how to change your life. But even if it succeeds in motivating you to make a fresh start, the rest might follow. A journey cannot be completed unless the first step is taken, so get up and take that first step you've been holding yourself back from for so long.

ACKNOWLEDGEMENTS

I would like to thank all my friends, aunts, uncles, sisters, brothers, parents and grandparents who believed in me to make this possible, to my wife Vandna Sinha for having the patience during the entire phase of me bringing the book to life and special thanks to my friends Vishal Adsool and Shireen Quadri for being the guide through the journey of this book.

CONTENTS

THE CHILD WITHIN YOU

When you first came into this world, as a baby, you came with no prejudice, no sense of right and wrong, no sense of birth and death, and no sense of Fear.

You did not have any conceptions about the world you had opened your eyes to. You did not know what kind of beings were they, the ones you sensed around you, you did not know why they were here, you did not know what a relationship meant, or what the world had to offer you, with its people, its technology, other beings, and nature in all its multitudinous variety and might.

You were unaware of the role of emotions in your life. You did not know what it meant to be happy, to be sad, to being a winner or loser. You did not know what competition was, or what it meant "To be the Best".

You also did not know what you yourself were, or your purpose in this world. You had no idea what it was that you might offer the world in return for its enabling you to not only survive but also flourish and accomplish the purpose of your existence.

As you learnt to stand on your own feet, you began to explore the world, and you were admitted to the knowledge of 'Good and Bad' and 'Right and Wrong' by your parents and dear ones, and above all, you learnt to be fearless.

'No' was not a word in your dictionary. You always had the urge to see, feel, or try anything new that you came across–be it an idea or an experience. Nothing could cast a spell of fear on you, as your mind was free and impervious to negative feelings. '*No*' was always, its '*On*', and you attempted to reverse and defy every logic that stopped you from exploring what the world had to offer.

When others told you that you should not try something because you were too young for it, you did not listen. You went ahead anyway, because you wanted to explore it first hand, without worrying about whether you would be able to finish the task. You could do so because venturing into unknown territory was fun and not something to be fearful about.

The world seemed like a playground where fun was never–ending. And fearlessness was the chariot on which one rode into this playground, signalling the beginning of a '*Happy Life*'–happiness being nothing but the feeling generated by the fun moments that life offered you.

As you began to understand what was happiness and what was sadness, you decided that you wanted to be happy every single moment of your life and would attempt everything to make it possible.

The first jump from the bed and chairs, the first time you got up with a smile on your face after you fell, your feet carrying you to hitherto unexplored places, your never–ending questions to your dear ones, what were all of these? Well, these moments were the dots, and joining them was supposed to shape your future.

In your school days, when for the first time you faced the challenge of having to prove yourself in a naughty activity, you would be among the first ones to jump in, and never gave it a second thought.

When you were on the playground honing the skills of a sportsperson, your body did not let you down when you had to save a goal, stop a run, take a brilliant catch, or cross the post.

You now began identifying yourself as a winner when competing on any front, and when you lost, you worked even harder, sharpened your skills even further so as to be back as a winner the next time around, but what still drove you more was enjoying the act.

You never backed down from working harder or learning from failures or taking a hit on yourself and yet marching ahead, your '*Will Power*' was stronger than any wall blocking your path. No matter that your fist was already bleeding — You kept on punching till it finally broke down.

Victory was precious to you but it was achieved through sheer hard work and effort, not via short cuts where your principles had to be compromised. 'Right' had begun to be differentiated from 'Wrong'. Your heart of gold was beating unfazed by the intoxications existing in the world. The mind and the heart could not be corrupted as they were not two separate entities but woven into one, and could not be affected by any thought or feeling pushed on to you by others.

When you rode your bicycle, you flew, showcasing your developing craziness as you took your hands off the handlebar, or balanced on one tyre, doing a wheelie while the world watched you in awe.

Trying something unconventional created a sense of higher satisfaction than falling in line and doing what was simply passed on. 'Oh that was awesome' presided over 'Do this as we all did this', and being different generated more sparkle in your eyes.

For you back then, everyone was your friend and dear to you. Religion, caste, family status and financial strength were concepts you never even bothered setting your mind to. You felt the utmost satisfaction in sharing what you had and were ever ready to lend your helping hand to anyone and everyone.

The categories of rich or poor, big or small, powerful or weak, did not guide your choice of friends and relationships — on it was the connection of hearts which did, telling you to go ahead with a new relationship.

The first impressions of education were not only your school books but also graphic novels, comics, and animated cartoons which brought you face to face with comic heroes and heroines, who then became your biggest idol in your growing up years. These were the kinds of people you wanted to become someday as a grown up, and you always wished you could become like them and help the world in its moments of need.

Traits which you developed while growing up have a high impact on what you ideally turn into when you step into adulthood. Furthermore, when, from being a responsibility of your parents, the roles are reversed and you become responsible for taking care of your parents and dear ones, your childhood idols matter.

The paths you then choose in your life, your career, your relationships, your entrepreneurship ventures, or your family business are bound to be guided by the choices you had made during your growing up years — the choices which were meant to make you '*HAPPY*'.

You wanted to change the world, touch lives, make a mark, and build your own identity–an identity which the world could look up to and admire.

Every festival, and occasions like birthday were eagerly looked forward to as you would get new clothes to wear, different dishes to eat, and meet your friends and relatives. The amount of joy you derived from that one day was plenty.

But as you grew up, what started happening? Well, fearlessness gave way to fear. You started getting self–conscious and confused at every decision, at every turn of life. You found yourself struggling to keep up in the rat race, — you didn't know when you first got into it, and there seemed to be no way of winning it or coming out of it to create your own world. You started differentiating among people, became more and more selfish, and, having lost the courage to make your own separate identity, wanted to join the herd at any cost.

Winning at any cost was your only motive, and the kind of short cuts you had ignored as a child started to become your first choice as an adult. Your heart of gold began to get corrupted and the heart and the mind became separate entities again, with the mind having the final say in decision–making.

The heart became a mere organ supporting life, and not the guiding angel which had showed you the path when you were a child.

In your job, you get the feeling that your salary is not sufficient given the rate of inflation. Every time you sit down with your colleagues and friends, you crib that you will quit the job and start your own business so that you can earn more and realise your dream of buying a house of your own, a sedan, and so on. Those who already have a business of their own, on the other hand, crib that the customer today has become more demanding than ever, and that more often than not you don't get the payment on time and you start feeling that you should wrap up your business venture and take up a job so that at least there is an assured income at the end of every month.

Whatever situation you are in, you are only cribbing that your present life is not going well and you want to run away from it. But is this happening with everyone around you, or are there still a few people of your age in jobs, or in business who are earning better and doing better and making their dreams come true? And even if the whip of inflation is still swinging high, have managed to move in a different direction or at least out of the range of the whip?

The moments which used to generate happiness and joy have evaporated into thin air. Perhaps you do not look forward to festivals anymore because now you can buy a new dress whenever you want, or can eat a variety of dishes anytime you want. So these special moments lose their value in your life since they are now easier to find, or the case may be that you no longer look forward to inviting guests to your house for fear of disrupting the finances for the month.

The whole purpose of your existence, which once upon a time used to be to make the world a better place and spread joy and happiness, has now changed — to one of survival and winning at any cost.

Take a deep breath, close your eyes, and look deep inside your inner conscience. You might soon realise that you are born only once as what you are, that your life needs to be valued, and its purpose in the world fulfilled, because that is what the balance of nature says. Nature is in an unbalanced state more than ever now, and there are only a handful who are trying to restore the balance. It is one's responsibility to support them and join them to restore the balance of nature to make this world a better place for the generations to come.

Nothing will bring you more closer to the goal of restoring nature's balance than and fulfilling the '*Purpose*' of your life than the child within you because it still has the purity of nature's innocence in his/her heart — the heart of gold.

Do not let your child get lost among the grownups ever again, as being happy is more valuable than merely surviving. Recall the key moments while you were growing up and you will be clear again what shape your life has to take from now on. Take the reins of the chariot of your life again in your hands, and march towards the purpose of your existence. Make a vow to lead a happy life and spread joy and happiness in the world from this moment on.

CURIOSITY: THE DESIRE TO EXPLORE

When you were born and opened your eyes in this world, your eyes seemed to wander in the universe around. There was no reason or association with the meanings the universe had to offer but the eyes still continued to wander in the empty and alien space.

No one knew what those wandering eyes of yours were looking for. The meaning of the gaze could not be interpreted, but everyone believed themselves to be the object of the gaze. People believed that your eyes were trying to recognise who they were, but in reality your gaze never stopped at any one person but kept on wandering even further into the universe.

Every time your gaze stopped at someone, the person got delighted that you are trying to associate with them, and when the gaze was accompanied by a smile, the person felt like a king or queen at that moment, and on cloud nine.

Your gaze could bring about smiles, tears of happiness, and emotions from even the toughest of persons as your gaze seemed to form a connection with them from the very first moment it looked at them.

But it was not meaning or a specific purpose that was guiding the turning of the head or the rotation of the eyes. And yet it went on and on and on and it seemed to be imprinting the images around in your mind.

As you progressed in the journey of this world, the wandering eyes started having an aim, a reason, and a question and started deciphering the universe around. There seemed to be a query in the wandering eyes always, trying to understand everyone and everything around.

Every tap to the body, every instance of being carried in the arms, every act of affection and care had the eyes in motion, exploring the entities around and interpreting the meaning of each act.

The universe was being unravelled and everything and everyone began to have a name for you. Your parents became 'Mom' and 'Dad'; your grandparents became 'Grandmother' and 'Grandfather'. Other relations began falling into nomenclatures like 'Sister', 'Brother', 'Uncle', 'Aunt', and so on.

The gaze now started projecting an association as it also had the power of the grunt from your throat to express your emotions and your approval or disapproval of the associations that seemed to form.

And as the epitome of curiosity gained legs, the universe began expanding and its associations with the world increased. From gaze to grunt to now the feet carrying you into the world, your ways of associating with everything and everyone reached a different level altogether as now you were not bound within the boundaries which had always been around you but ready to take on the world and challenge its limits. You became unstoppable.

Every toy, every person, every room, every gadget, every material was explored with the utmost curiosity to understand its association with you. You began identifying entities beyond your mother and father like 'My Home', 'My toy', 'My dress', 'My shoes', 'My Sister', 'My friend' and so on and the list began running into pages.

The mind was active, always making a meaning of everything. The questions started emerging every now and then, "What is This", "Why this is used", "How this is used"," Can I use it", "Can I eat it", "Can I touch this" and so on, the dictionary of curiosity started building up.

You were curious to know about everything, from the world, to the universe, to the people, to the animals, to your family, to your house, everything you could see and feel.

Do you remember the moments when you would detach the head of your toy and look for what's inside the body of the toy or when you would get into the arms of your dear ones for ringing the door bell and feel excited by its sound?

When you used to go to your parents' office or their business premises, you were curious to know how each machine worked, how records were maintained, what was everyone's job, and so on.

What about the paper boats you floated, and were amazed by when they vanished in a few seconds, or the balloons that, when you let them go, drifted into the clouds, leaving you staring endlessly at the sky, thinking about where they went and hoping they would be back in your hands soon.

You used to be a creative chef mixing various dishes every time to create something new — a soft drink of one taste and style was mixed with that of another type to create a new drink, a new homemade mocktail from your personal kitchen. Sweet gravy in your dinner was mixed with spicy gravy to create new sweet–spicy gravy and so on.

That was the time when someone offered a closed fist and asked you to guess what was inside; your imagination ran from toffee to sweets to even the weirdest of options such as the moon, the stars, and so on.

You attempted to operate the remote of television with your tiny little fingers and generated a roar of joy when in your attempt you realised that the display on the television screen was changing as your fingers operated the buttons. Though you did not associate the numerals on the buttons to the changes on the TV screen — say, channel number 9 was a cartoon channel, you did not know how to click the buttons to arrive at channel 9, but still on your click any change in the display produced moments of joy for you and if in the series of clicks, the channel showing your favourite cartoon appeared, you stopped there and were happy and became glued to the television.

If any guest came to your house, you would peep in from behind the curtain to see who the person was, with an eye also on what was in the serving utensil which was served to the guest. You felt shy to come in front of the guest but once your parents introduced you and you were offered a bite from the plate by the guest, they became close to you and all the shyness disappeared.

When a new toy was gifted to you, you attempted to break it down into parts, and once you were able to do that, you attempted to put the parts back together. Even though you failed to get your toy up and running again, still, when you got another toy, you would again attempt to dismantle it as your mind was not tired of trying to find out everything about anything you could lay hands on.

You may remember the attempt to insert your hand in the table fan or the electric switch board, and thanks to your guardians and parents for keeping an eye on you, you were stopped from doing so. Yet when they took you away from the fan or the switch board, your head looked back, attempting to demystify the rotating blades of the fan or the dark space of the electrical sockets.

You may remember biting into the lipsticks used by your mother as you were fascinated by its vibrant colour and smell and wanted to find out what it tasted like. You may remember your attempt to touch the lighted matchstick or the fire on the gas burner or a candle flame. You wanted to know about everything and anything which pressed your curiosity button.

But when you grew up and entered your professional life, your married life, your educational life, things gradually began to change. Your eyes stopped wandering around with a question in them, and your mind stopped thinking and exploring, and instead, accepted everything as it was presented to you.

Your gaze was stuck in one direction and seemed meaningless. The eyes were staring into a hollow space and the mind, rather than producing meaning, had shut down its operation and was in a zombie like state.

Even when made to participate in a discussion, the moment the topic shifted to avenues unknown to you, rather than being curious to know about it, you chose to bring yourself out of the discussion, citing some excuse that there was something else you just remembered you had to attend to.

Newspapers and books were read only for topics which were of your interest or to pass an examination and not to enlighten yourself on the new developments in the world. Rather than being the one to start something new, you chose to use or work on what was passed on by those who dared to think different and change the world.

From being an inventor, you became an end user. From being an interrogator of conventions, you became someone content to receive readymade answers without even questioning the authenticity of the answers you received.

You stopped dismantling the toys and gadgets as they were now being bought for basic usage and were meant to serve a purpose and not act as objects to play with.

You took up your education and career just as a continuation of the legacy your elders passed onto you, without attempting to explore new avenues or new career options. Your brain was tied up in conventional thoughts on the subject of education. You took up the known path you had seen your elders taking earlier, because they seemed easier for your mind to interpret and understand, and offered you the security of the known and the familiar.

The jobs you took up post education were based on what was present in abundance and was comparatively easier to get into. A new line of job, something which was not famous or where vacancies were not present in abundance you avoided and did not even attempt to gain a basic insight into.

You became a part of the assembly line education format which was generating products instead of visionaries who could have the power to change the world by their efforts and determination. Jobs became mere means of survival and not the path towards fulfilment of the purpose of life.

You continued with the same style of functioning to run your family business, without even thinking about new ideas to suit the demands of the changing times, or trying to come up with ideas which could have really rocketed your business to the next level.

When you managed to gather the courage to start a fresh business, sometimes against the wishes of your dear ones, you chose to take up something which was not new and did not have an innovative approach–which would have been necessary to break free of the already established market dynamics. So the venture did not last long and its failure not only hurt you economically but also dented your spirit to take on the world on your own terms ever again.

And if you are already in the setting years of your life, then post–retirement, you might have a feeling that life is already over for you, and all you might be doing now is counting days as you might feel that you do not have it in you anymore to enjoy life and your time is almost over.

You just somehow wanted to survive rather than make a name for yourself, or create a meaning for your life, or fulfil the purpose of your life. You started taking every day as the same day, every moment as the same moment–something which was not in your control but guided by your destiny only.

But what is wrong with this — with not exploring, and not being curious? Well let's see what has happened. You have started to find your life becoming monotonous, your jobs and personal lives becoming boring and frustrating, and you find yourself cursing yourself for having made wrong life choices. And all your curses are aimed primarily at the system and the people around you rather than yourself.

Let anyone ask you to do a task that is beyond your daily routine chore and see how you react with frustration. You may eventually end up doing that task, but with a lot of grumblings so that the person who gave you the work gets the hint that you do not like to be given extra work. Say, your spouse asks you to buy groceries from the market, an activity which she used to perform on her own without involving you but this time she has asked you to do this chore on a Sunday. You will immediately throw a tantrum, and start off about how busy a person you are, that it's only on Sundays that you get to relax, and how you do not like to handed over chores like this.

In reality, the task is not that big that it will throw your routine or your plans for the rest of the day out of the window. But you still crib as your mind is not ready to accept anything beyond your monotonous routine.

You might have consulted astrologers to do all sorts of rituals to somehow change the path your destiny was taking you. In your eyes your life was solely being guided by your fate, and you have no control over it. Naturally, the only person who you thought could influence your destiny was the astrologer. You did not even realise that any ritual might work provided you too make the effort in the right direction to initiate the change you have been hankering for, for a long time.

When you compete against others in your job, as you see the number of your competitors increasing with every passing day, your heart sinks. You get easily demoralised because, now that you have turned into a product created on an assembly line and not the explorer you once were, you find it tough to differentiate yourself from the competition.

And what do you do then? Once again you curse your job, your life, the people around you who seem to be having an edge over you, your superiors, the system, and once you are back home, the ultimate recipient of your curses are the parents who raised you and got you to this level. But now you curse them for not having done better than what they did for your education and career, and the final object of your wrath is your spouse whom you suddenly begin to falsely visualise as someone not supportive enough of you in your struggling moments.

From being the centre of your life, they overnight become the prime reason why you are not excelling, and you start pinpointing their shortcomings, forgetting all that they have done, and are still doing, to make you happy.

You curse your parents for your stagnating career, blaming them for not having given you the best possible education–for not having sent you to the best school or college, while ignoring their efforts and sacrifices to get you the level of education that they did, for even that was something they could barely afford, but were able to manage only by using the same set of clothes for years, driving the same old two–wheeler for god knows how long, eating the same type of food every time and so on. You curse your spouse, imagining that because of him or her you are struggling in your job. You start branding them as 'Unlucky', or assert that they have been a negative influence on you from the day they set foot in your life, without realising that it was their dreams and life too that is being shattered when you curse them and their parents. The dreams which they had–of leading a happy married life with you–are broken, and they cease to occupy in your heart the special place that used to be theirs. The world around, made up of your friends and dear ones, suddenly seems like a world mocking you for your failures even if in reality they happen to be genuinely interested to help you and support you. You begin drifting away from all your well-wishers, sinking even deeper into depression. And the quicksand of depression is such that you feel that the only way to proceed is to getting deeper into it. Your whole life becomes a struggle, and every breath is like torture.

Your closed mind has not only closed the doors of success for you but also closed the avenues of happiness as everyone around you is now drifting away from you, and from having been a crowd–puller–which you were when you were born — you have somehow turned into a loner.

You start becoming an example of failure, a warning for the people around you, the one from whom growing up kids should learn what not to do or what not to become in their lives when they grow up in few years' time. Rather than becoming a role model, you become a model of 'What you should not become'. You become the laughing stock not only for the people around you but also for those who were once your friends.

You are slowly weeded out from the group of 'Achievers' — either by virtue of not being informed of or invited to gatherings, or being flatly told on the face that you should now avoid being a part of their group.

You almost drag yourself to work every day now; Monday Blues is turning out to be true to its name not only on Mondays but on every single day that you report to work. It has engulfed even your Sundays and holidays now as your frustrations do not choose days any more but erupt at any moment.

Your office mood spells over into your personal life, and the time which you could have utilised to engage in generating joy by enjoying with your family gets destroyed. You do not find joy in anything or with anyone any more as your mind is too preoccupied with depressing thoughts about the situation you are in.

Is it really the system that is responsible for this frustration? Are you too not a part of the system that is creating this frustration? Why exactly does your work and your life seem so boring, monotonous and frustrating? Well, one of the realities is that your mind has stopped exploring and being curious, and therefore, you are bound to accept everything even if you don't like it.

You continue to lead life the way others and the system want you to, not realising that it was your choice to be a part of the system, and therefore only you have the power to change it.

Your worries are based on your choices. You therefore cannot pass on the blame to the ones around you and to the system. Your choice of higher education, your efforts to excel in it, your choice of job, and your efforts to excel in it were made by you, so you cannot blame others solely. Your mind has to explore the world for what benefits you and no one else can play that ultimate role of explorer for you.

It's like this: if you feel thirsty, you drink the water to quench the thirst, and your body and its systems make an effort to absorb the water and bring you comfort. But if someone else drinks the water, it will quench not your thirst but theirs. Similarly, in this case as well, the effort to change your situation lies solely in your hands and in no one else's. Others can guide you towards a path they feel might be the best for you, but in the end, it is you who has to walk the path, and based on your efforts, make your life worth living.

There is a saying, 'Rules are meant to be bent or broken'. As a child, you always saw the world from your eyes, and your perspective of it came from your own thinking, without being prejudiced by what the system had to offer you. The system was there just as a point of reference. The real meaning was interpreted by your mind and heart and their explorations took you beyond the visible boundaries.

But how do you break these rules again? How to gain back the moments of happiness for you and your dear ones? Well, one way to do this is to Awake the child within you. This will unshackle your mind again, open your eyes to the world around, guide your search for answers, for ways to change the system, and ultimately change your life for good, bring about the transformation which is most important for a human being — more even than mere survival.

When was the last time you tried dismantling a machinery or a toy to understand how it works based on what your learned in the book of machines? Well, it is time you became a "Mechanic" again.

The important step now is to start reading, and reading does not mean only what you like but topics beyond that. Many of you will say that you read a lot as it is your hobby to read novels, and so on. But does that really address the need to explore?

You must move beyond what you read for fun and start reading books and other materials online or offline about subjects beyond your hobbies and begin bending your mind again. Even as you make this effort — at this very moment, with this book in your hand — make a pledge that you will continue reading and expanding your horizon of knowledge henceforth.

Increasing your knowledge base will let you determine your future course of action by which you will be able to make your choices consciously and not merely because the system is thrusting them on you. For example, while learning about a computer–related subject, a person may discover that he actually likes it–a liking he was not aware of before as he did not have adequate knowledge about this field. But now he is aware about this new field, and his liking for it, may open up a new avenue for, say, a person from the banking sector. So, if this person had been in a banking job that he was unhappy and frustrated with, he may shift to the IT sector based on his new liking, and this might allow happiness to once again seep back into his work life, and also impact his personal life positively.

This may enable you to change the system based on your choice, and start your career afresh with a revived zeal.

Next, learn a new language. A new language presents such an alien structure to the mind that it will have to bend a lot to grasp it. The process of learning it will enable you to look at the world from a different perspective as, along with the vocabulary of the new language, you will also learn about the lives and culture of the people who speak that language as their mother tongue, and this whole new perspective will have an indirect impact on your job too.

As a child, you might have created a new language known only to your friends, with new words and a new meaning for every word. This may have served as a secret code language for your intimate circle of friends when you had to pass on an important message to them even when there were others around you. This was fun, right? Well, along with being fun, it was also an exposure for your mind to parts unknown.

The world is fast getting globalised today. Say you are in a job which has exposure to international markets and you attempt to learn a new language, say French. Now, if any project is assigned to your department by French clients, then you might stand a better chance to grab a spot on the team handling that project as your superiors will find your acquaintance with the language an added advantage while servicing French customers. This may help you build advantage vis–a–vis your peers as your experience in international projects will put your graph on a higher level. All this, in turn, will generate greater satisfaction and happiness for you.

If you are in a business or an entrepreneurial venture, start reading about other ventures that have made it big and, if possible, meet their leaders and see how you can learn from them, how they do not think only about surviving but also choose to think beyond convention by expanding the business in various other lines, coming out with various innovative products, and so on. Don't get bogged down by the feeling that no one will give you their precious time. First read up about the person on the internet, and then approach him/her through a contact in your immediate circle. And even if you do not have such contacts, it might not matter, for if the person is someone who believes in changing the world, he or she might still be ready to give you some of their precious time provided you have the patience to wait for their Yes.

If you are a retired person, then go out, take up new voluntary assignments, or enrol in a course of higher education, either by correspondence or part time, and start learning and bending your mind and thought processes again. Take an interest in the latest gadgets your children and grandchildren use and learn to operate them, or maybe join them in playing the latest games on their TV consoles and see how you can finish all the levels, pushing your mental stamina to the limit. So awaken the child within you and reignite the flame of curiosity. Doing so will empower you to take control of the system and change it to your liking, generating happy moments again.

BEING FEARLESS

When you first tried to use your feet, what happened was that you stood up but immediately you fell down. If you ask your parents and guardians about what happened next, without any surprise, the answer would be that you stood up again to take the next step. And mind you, the next step was with the same smile on your face, same spark in your eyes, and the same zeal to move on.

What was this act? Well, this act was of defiance, an act which signalled to the world that come what may, you will not back down; if it brings you to earth, you will rise again like the phoenix and build your life on your terms.

It was a challenge to the situation you were into and you were announcing to the world that 'I am stronger than any wall that is raised in front of me; I will climb on it, break it, and make my own way'.

This spirit was nothing else but the spirit of being fearless. Nobody could scare you, or generate a sense of the impossible within you, and everything you could see or visualize and take up a fight to, seemed always possible.

'*Impossible*' for you was always interpreted as '*I Am Possible*'. There was nothing which you could abandon without trying. Failure was not an option for you. All you knew was that you have to do it and you gave it your best shot to accomplish it.

People around you at times gave a note of caution when you attempted to do something which seemed tough in their eyes. But you laughed at the sight of the task at hand and went ahead to break it down and conquer it.

How many of you roamed in the house with a towel on your back enacting the life of a comic book hero or heroine — the whole feeling of you, too, being a comic hero or comic heroine made you feel invincible at that age, made you the most powerful being you have known of, the one who could confront and defeat any challenge.

As a child, whatever the situation you were faced with, the first feeling was not to run away from it, but to ignite the spirit of the comic book hero/heroine within you and confront it with higher intent, with no sense of fear or even the remotest feeling of getting defeated.

From all those sudden fights you got into — from situations of passing an exam which was not your subject of interest, to catching the insects with your bare hands (a sight which always scared your mothers), to being ready to embark on any journey your friends wanted you to be a part of (even in the early hours of the morning or when you went on so-called ghost trails late at night), to facing any situation with open arms and a sparkle in your eye, it was the spirit of fearlessness which enabled you to handle any situation and stand up for what you believed in.

As a child, you too would have had your own share of fights. But do you remember yourself running away from the scene, or did you pull up the sleeves of your shirt and got ready to tackle the fight head on even if you at that moment were outnumbered by your opposition? There was no one or nothing which could strike fear in your heart as you always felt invincible and believed in yourself.

And if you are a guy then you would remember that if the fight was for the girl you had a crush on, then every punch on your face was faced by you with open arms and with a smile on your face as you knew that you were about to get an opportunity to gather her attention and affection. There was no place for fear as your heart had only her image showing sympathy and showering affection towards you. (Okay, take your time and remember all those moments before you proceed reading further.)

Now continue with the smile on your face and recall the time you held a lit candle in your hand and swung your fingers to and fro in the fire on the tip of the candle. You had always been taught to stay away from fire but you still attempted to play with it as your heart was not scared by the sight of fire on the candle tip and instead, wanted to tame it.

Remember climbing to the highest point on the mango tree to pluck mangoes? Even the sight of the thinnest or the weakest branch would not deter you from reaching the shining mango you had set your eyes on. And what about the time when the mango tree you were on did not belong to you but to your neighbour who on seeing you came running after you with a stick in his hand, but rather than realizing your mistake, you still went back again, hiding from the neighbour, and climbed on the tree again the very next day or may be the same evening?

This act might not be right in the spirit of morality but this is one of those few transgressions which almost everyone remembers having committed as children, when they, rather than being scared, had fun in attempting the dare again and again.

Those who went to boarding schools would remember the time they went out of the hostel gate into the market place and while returning, if they got late, how they jumped over the boundary wall, hurried to their rooms in darkness and wrapped themselves in the blanket as though they had been sleeping there for hours.

The warden may have issued clear instructions on the very first day itself that such acts will invite punishments. But you still defied the rules occasionally as your heart did not understand the meaning of fear. Instead, it revelled in breaking some small rules — all so that you could boast about it to your friends and raise your value in their eyes and be envied by everyone else for having been able to enjoy something which they could not even dream of being able to.

When the whole world was against your friends, you stood by them, guarding them and shielding them from everyone else. You dared to take all the curses falling on them upon yourself and would stand firm and not let your foot be dragged even one step behind the line. No one could defeat you when you stood for what was right as you were powered by the spirit of invincibility.

When you committed a mistake, you accepted its consequences once you realized that it was your mistake and you were not scared to be punished for it as you vowed never to repeat it again.

During the school days, when your friend alone was caught for any prank that your group had played together, you too stood up and offered yourself up voluntarily when the punishment was being meted out as you not only had the daring to commit a prank but also the strong heart to accept your role in it. You were not scared of the consequences it would lead up to as you always considered yourself to be strong enough to handle any situation you were put into.

Remember the time you wrote a letter to your love interest with your proposal and walked up to him/her and handed over the letter in person? Your heart was not scared of the consequences. Instead it prayed and hoped that the answer would be '*Yes*'. This act required a great amount of courage as it directly affected your emotions and feelings and was not just a game where you could come back and win again. It was an instance where victory or defeat was on the spot, with rare second chances. You were not someone who would run away but a mass of power which was forever ready to stand and face the system and give it its best shot to overpower it.

But over the years, from being someone who always faced any given situation and stared it back in the eye, you turned into someone who would lower his/her eyes, turned the face sideways, and submitted to the situation. The comic hero or heroine has taken a back seat and is no more to be seen. What is seen now is the changed '*You*' which is no more the phoenix waiting to rise again but the escapist.

During the school days, in the recess you would run to get hold of the swing or the slides and would enjoy on it endlessly. But if now you have an opportunity to get onto the swing again, you will suddenly have a nauseating feeling. You might think, 'I can't do this now, I would feel dizzy.' Are you so weak now that a swing on which little kids play around endlessly would have a deadly impact on your health even if you sat on it for few seconds?

Whenever you find yourself in a situation you are not comfortable with, say, a work profile which seems to be very demanding and not of your interest, or a project which demands more than what you know currently, or a marital relationship which requires that you submit to it totally, or relationships that you don't have your heart in, such as with certain friends and relatives, your impulse seems to be to back off, to try to run away.

The invincible smile on the face has given way to an expression of a scared being that might shout and jump in fear even if a mouse squeaks.

When someone in your workplace tries to take the credit for your work, rather than fight for your right, you now accept it as your fate and fight only to survive in the job–putting up with it even if others rise in the corporate ladder based on *your* efforts. You end up cursing your fate, your colleagues, your superiors, and your very own life.

When you are suddenly asked a question in an interview or by your superior in front of others and you do not know the answer to it, you still try to scramble up an answer and are scared to say 'I don't know', in the belief that saying that might ruin your chances of landing the job or the project. This belief ties in with your mind-set that in any case you are now only fighting to survive and not to excel and be happy.

When your superior at work calls you and your peers for a monthly/regular performance review, your heart sinks. You start praying that your boss does not ask you questions or evaluate you in that meeting. Rather than being confident of your performance, you are scared of being picked on and blasted for your shortcomings. You feel that your flaws may not even be under your control as you have lost your confidence and are in no position to defend yourself any more. Fear of the '*Unknown*' has now been amplified by the fear of the '*Known*' as you now anticipate what might be about to happen.

Your juniors no longer look up to you as their leader and mentor, as someone who will guide their career path, as by being afraid to take risks you might be ruining their chances to grow and prosper in the organization. Your failure to perform has repercussions also on the performance of your team as a team is recognized primarily by its leader and you have failed to inspire them.

Say you and your team have been handed over a project by the management and your superiors but to drive it you need to make certain decisions at your end. But because you are scared, you fail to take the crucial calls and pass on the project's entire responsibility to your team. With their limited exposure to the magnitude of the project and limited approach to the required resources and support required to run it, your team is unable to take a decision or back the decision taken with some concrete background to support it, so even if you take the decision or leave it on your team to take it, the project fails, putting in jeopardy the career prospect of the entire team.

When you are running a business and need to take a risk, to, say, buy new types of equipment or machinery which have just come into the market, then, rather than going ahead with buying it, you are scared to be the first to test the waters. You choose to wait for it to settle down in market, and thereby lose the edge your company might have had if it had taken the risk of being the first mover.

Let's say, as an entrepreneur, you have to decide on whether or not to take up a project which offered high returns but was from a subject which was not among your strengths. Even when you were in real need of good customers and good sales, rather than sharpening the skill set required, you avoided taking on the risky project as you were scared of the clauses that might come into force in case the project was not completed as per the requirements. For any new business, getting business development is really tough and will always demand a high level of risk–taking, more than what you might have to take when you are employed somewhere. But now, since you are scared to get into unknown territories, you will avoid them even if you had the potential to make them a success. It is fear that takes over.

As you grow old, you are scared to even take decisions for your family. You feel that times have changed and now it's your children who will be the ones taking decisions, even for your well being.

These might seem to be instances of varying magnitude but they still add up to amplifying the fear being generated and solidifying in your heart, and the fear is one that cannot be melted away with ease any more.

When you commit a mistake, rather than accepting it, now you build a series of lies around it so that it does not affect your job prospects. And what about the lies you are committing in the relationship with your spouse and dear ones? You are scared to accept your mistake here as well, as for you the prime importance is for the relationship to survive even if its base is weakened by the sands of lies. You have lost the courage to walk up to your spouse and dear ones and apologize for the mistake you have committed. Rather you create an imaginary world in their eyes where you project everything to be under your control when in reality you have become a slave to the situation.

When your children ask you about your job and your current life, you tend to lie to them, build false stories of how good your life is running, and how great your achievements are in your job as you are scared of being projected as a 'Loser' rather than a 'Hero' or 'Heroine' in their eyes, given that they are bound to look up to you and would wish to be like you some day. When you were young, your parents took you to their offices sometimes and showed you around as they felt a sense of pride in showcasing their achievements to you. Do you take your children that often to your office now to show them around? It is highly probable that the answer to this question would be 'No'. What has changed now from the time when you visited your parent's offices? Does work not have the same relevance now as it did in the time of your parent's working life?

Today, when you have filled the shoes of your parents and taken up their role of an idol in your children's lives, you just can't be the same as what they were to you. The big difference in your life at work as compared to that of your parents is that it's now only about survival for you and no more about a sense of pride which you can showcase to your children. You are scared that you might lose the tag of 'role model' in their lives now if they get to see the real picture of you — the picture of a loser, the sorry face of a scared being, the one who has forgotten how to live to inspire any one. The truth will get exposed by the questions your children might ask you once they are at your workplace, say, about your name missing from the table of achievers pasted in the office, or they might throw some questions at you which you might not be comfortable answering as the reality might be different from what you had been telling your kids at home.

When your children ask you questions on various topics, say, when they ask you to show how a gadget works, you immediately push them away, saying that you are busy and don't have time and will attend to them later once you are free. But this free time in reality never comes as you are scared to reveal to your children that there could be topics you might also not be aware of despite being older than them and being their all–knowing parents. And mind you, you do have a chance to learn about these topics and then later on coming back to them with the answers to their queries. But since you are scared that you may not be able to learn the new subject well and that there may be still questions you might not have answers to, you let that chance go in vain–a chance that you could have used to get closer to your children and strengthen your bonds with them.

When your employees in your business, on getting a new project, ask you how to go ahead with it, rather than learning about the new project and guiding them, you push them to learn about it on their own as you are scared that in case you turn out to be incompetent in front of them, you might lose face.

Even as an ageing parent, you hesitate to speak your mind out as you are bogged down by what's happening in the world around where the children do not stay with their parents any more once they get old, and so you feel that your dated thinking might push them away from you.

Fear has crept in every aspect of your life. Moments which were under your control when you were children are no longer so. You have lost the reins of the chariot of those moments in your life now. Your courage has become so fragile that even a hint of fear shatters it into countless pieces.

As a child, you believed in execution first. You did not worry too much about consequences. Your courage ruled over your feelings of confusion. The fear of the unknown was non–existent. In fact, you constantly sought exciting moments when you could challenge the limits of your might again. Today, exactly the opposite is happening. You first make calculations on the probability of getting expected results, and you act only when you find the bet to be safe — rather than going ahead based on your instincts. In other words, you have stopped growing because, as you very well know, high risk brings in high returns, and this is the principle which dictates the pace at which your life grows.

What happens then is that either your output is below required expectations, or you leave the work in hand and get into something else which might turn out to be even worse than what was the case in the first place. You change your work profiles, your jobs, and even get into industries or work profiles which demand totally different attributes from what you are good at or been educated in. You go on creating differences with your spouses, your families and friends and over a period of time, rather than getting closer to each other, you start drifting away at an uncontrolled pace. You in the end become a slave to the situation rather than overpowering it. The powerful has become powerless.

People start taking you for granted, tagging you as a 'loser', and taking undue advantage of you and your skills. When you are assigned any work in a group, you might find others taking it easy while you yourself are slogging to complete the task, and when the evaluation happens, they take the major share of the success, while you have lost the courage to even fight for your rightful due.

And what if the profile you are in is something you are not good at, if it is different from what you excelled in over the years and built your base on? Then the situation is even worse as you have lost the confidence that you too can learn something new at this junction of your life. You are scared that the time lost in learning the new skill sets might hamper your survival in the job. So you close your mind and slog day–in and day–out to meet just the basic criteria of surviving in that job.

Well, if you study it carefully, fear has not only become a part of your professional life but also crept into your personal life without you even noticing it. You begin to run away from every situation that you find challenging or pushes you to the wall.

Say, when you make a promise to your spouse to do something out of the way but are unable to do it, the first reaction you have is that you did not have time to do it, though you hadn't even given it a try. But if the '*No Time*' cry is ignored and you are pressed hard by your spouse, then rather than promising to take up the challenge again and this time with a strong heart, you again run away from it by either expressing your '*No–Logic*' frustration to them or by moving away from the conversation and the scene where the challenge is grilled into a promise.

Rather than taking the responsibility for not delivering on your promise you end up looking for loop holes. You start blaming your spouse for your not having kept your promise, or divert the topic of conversation to a different plane where you can easily pinpoint mistakes committed by your spouse.

The courage to accept your mistakes has now given way to the need to satisfy the ego. So you attempt to gain the upper hand by putting your spouse down for the mistakes he or she may have committed. You shift the topic– from the conflict that needs to be resolved now, to something else that may have happened earlier and has no relevance in the present situation. You do it because you feel the need to show that you are the one in command, that it is you who is in the driver's seat in this relationship. And besides, you are scared to lose the hollow authority you have been exercising over your spouse for so many years.

You start running away from every moment; from every task and every person that scares you as you are afraid of failing again. You fear that your failure will reaffirm your position in the eyes of those around you as someone you never want yourself to be projected as–a loser. But in reality, there is no end to running away. If you run away from your current situation, there will be something else ready to emerge and attack you again, scaring you to the core. Do you really want to be running away all your life? Do you want to be tagged as a loser?

And so, as time passes, you grow bitter. You begin to curse the system again every single day, you curse your fate, and you start to believe that the world is not kind to you. But then, have you ever paused to ask yourself why the world should be kind to you? The world commands the beings that are weak and takes control of their lives while bowing to, and taking orders from, the ones who command it by their acts of courage and valour day in and day out.

You will say that the people around you are not good and that is why you are suffering. You will argue that your spouse is not supportive and that is why you are suffering, or that your friends are all selfish and leave you alone in your moments of need and that is why you are suffering. You will have similar nonsensical logic to explain every trouble you are going through. You do everything except take responsibility for your suffering and acknowledge to yourself that you are suffering because you have lost the courage to fight for your own rights, and that you are too scared to lead the life of your ideals and instead lead the life the world is pushing you towards.

The valiant 'Hero' or 'Heroine' who was not scared of anyone or anything has now been replaced with a 'Slave', a slave of the situation and the system who can only take orders from every one and from life instead of making his/her own mark based on his/her courage and valour. Fear has seeped into every decision, every thought, and every act in your life.

There is a saying, '*FEAR* is the absence of strength.' You may recall that when you were a child, every pore of your body and soul was brimming with strength. There was no space for fear to creep in. You were strongly in control of your life and followed your instinct and gut to take decisions, and to take action to achieve what you had set your eyes on.

The 'Hero' or 'Heroine' was alive and kicking in your heart and mind, ready to take on any task the world or the system had to offer. Just the look of determination on your face compelled the system to bend itself to suit your requirements. You instilled fear in the heart of the system pushing it, conveying the clear message that if it did not bend to your will, it would be shattered by your courage.

But how do you embrace such strength again, get rid of your fears, and be the 'Hero' or 'Heroine' again? The world should be what you make of it and not what it makes of you; the system should be back to following your orders and not ordering you to take the steps that impact your life.

The most important thing is to stand up to the situation and not give up without giving your best. If the work at hand or the situation demands knowledge that you do not possess, then explore, and get yourself into a better frame of mind in order to be able to face it. It's always wise to know about the enemies' strength, but wiser to understand their weaknesses and attack them there.

There is no end to learning. It's said that in our entire lives we use only a small percentage of our brain capacity, which means that a huge part of it still remains unused. So why not activate it to its maximum potential? Learning is not bound by your age. If you look around you might still find retired senior citizens taking up lessons in painting or music, and joining classes to gather the expertise required to enjoy new forms of culture, thereby proving that age is not relevant when it comes to learning. You can keep on learning and gaining knowledge all your life provided you have the courage to accept that there is still scope for you to improve yourself.

Today the world is moving faster than ever. Every new technology that emerges as a disruptive innovation becomes obsolete in no time. When the landline phone technology came up, you learned how to operate it. When mobiles replaced them in your life, you again learned how to operate them. When smart phones entered the scene, you once again taught yourself how to use them. And now, it is the age of the tablet, and you have again learned how to operate them.

So when you can keep yourself updated with the latest changes in the world of mobile technology, why can't you replicate the same zeal in your work, and keep yourself updated on all the new trends that may have a direct impact on your job, and by mastering which you may acquire an edge over your peers?

Don't be scared of failure when mastering a new subject. Instead, take it up with passion and with an aim to excel in it. You are scared of the stigma that will attach itself to you if you take up something new and do not excel in it; you are afraid that you might become a laughing stock. But don't be scared of this feeling. Fight it out by bringing out your courageous self, and you will soon realize that you are improving your command over the subject. And in this process, you may acquire that much needed edge, which you need to excel in your work place.

Your next step will be to awaken in you again the spirit of the comic book hero or heroine. You can do this by promising to yourself every day that you will not back out and will overcome any situation. A promise made to the world can be easily broken but when you make a promise to your soul and remind yourself of it every day and every moment, then you are bound to stand up to protect it.

As a child you used to get up early on Sunday mornings to watch animated cartoon shows of your favourite comic book heroes or heroines. You would recite their dialogues endlessly. Now you have the power of the internet at your disposal. Watch the old cartoon videos again to pump up your courage. This will not come to you easily or naturally, so try and convince yourself of this every day till you are sure of it.

When you are faced with any so called tough situation at work or in your personal life, don't be scared of the negative consequences. Instead, face them with a positive spirit, look deep inside yourself and make a promise to yourself that you will attempt to overcome the challenge with the courage that had always supported you when you were growing up. You shall remind yourself at every moment that you are stronger than the situation you are in, as you have the mace of courage with which to destroy the wall that's blocking the path to your better life, and you do not let even an iota of fear creep in at any moment.

In your personal life now, when you make a promise to your spouse and children, do not break it. Do not run away from the situation this time, Do everything which is in your control to fulfil your promise even if the situation has been pushed on to you by them and was not your choice in the first place. When you make a promise this time, hold their hands look into their eyes, and speak to them with a courageous heart.

At any given moment when you feel that you are getting weaker and are struggling to keep up the promise, remember how their faces looked while you were making your promise to them. This might work as a tonic that could save you from all your worries and provide you the spirit and strength to fight out the remaining battle and emerging victorious by fulfilling the promise you had made.

If, as an entrepreneur, you have an opportunity to bid for a big project, then this time may be, rather than playing it safe or running away from it because you feel that the competitors applying for the bid are stronger and bigger than you are, attempt to take a calculative risk and stretch yourself beyond your comfort zone. Go all out with renewed zeal to bag the project even if you have to work extra hours for the next few days or have to learn something altogether different from the subjects which you like. Be as innovative as you can when you present your case to the client. It's not always the case that only the biggest companies bag a deal. Even the most innovative idea might bag it. So do not restrain your thinking abilities and be a role model for your employees, so that they emulate your hard work and enthusiasm and give their best to make the project a success once it's been bagged.

Next, you need to utilize your spare time to give yourself opportunities to learn and excel in fields that are challenging. This requires courage because these ideally should be a field in which you are no longer interested and might therefore be tempted to avoid, saying that you '*Do Not Have Time For All This*'.

Say you always loved to play badminton as child and took on challenges from any one to defeat them in a game. Even if you suffered a defeat, you vowed to come back as a better player the next time around and take up the challenge again. Well, the time has come to get back in that game again.

People love challenges in their areas of interest as there is a sense of being in command that is attached to it. So it is a good idea to get back to the game of badminton or whatever other areas of interest that you had as a child. Join a club or become a part of a circle where people have retained these activities as a part of their lives and start going up against them.

Initially, success might be rare. You might be out of practice. You may not possess the framework and the courage of a fighter as the sense of fear has crept in your life. But don't surrender your weapons. Instead hold on to your fort now and every time you step on to the court, learn from your failures and start standing up to the challenges and give your improved best every time.

Soon you will realize that the sense of failure is giving way to a spirit of victory. And this could happen because rather than being a '*Escapist*' again on being defeated, you improved every time, took up the challenge, and finally began emerging victorious, thereby re–igniting in your heart the courage to take on any situation head on.

Next, make a commitment to giving an examination in a subject of your choice. There is no end to learning, and no end to the educational degrees you can hold. So explore what you can take up by managing the time you have on hand every day. Try to take up something which will have a direct impact on your job, or if you are retired, take up a subject which you missed taking up during your educational phase, as this will act as a much needed motivation for you to attempt something like this at this phase in your life. Give your time, your heart, and your soul to prepare for it. Once you start preparing for it on a regular basis and practicing with focus, slowly you will start realizing that the confidence which had eluded you for so long is coming back again, motivating you and pushing you to challenge your limits.

If you pass in the examination, it may have an immediate effect on your job, raising your level of performance and giving you a much needed edge against your peers. It will boost your confidence such that even at an advanced age, you still have it in you to excel in what you take up. But even if you do not perform well, still the required outcome would already have been achieved as the seeds of courage would have been re–sown in your heart.

And once the *Winner* emerges again within you, the spirit will not contain itself within the boundaries of your area of interest but expand to engulf every aspect of your life and every situation you that you face at work or at home or anywhere in the world.

And last but not the least; find the courage again to improve yourself as a person and a human. As a child you might have developed some bad habits, but then your dear ones would have guided you to let go of those bad habits and be a better person. But over the years this improving phase somehow ended as we did not felt its need as we grew up. We need to realize that we improve as a person all our lives, and therefore this process never stops. So gather the courage again and look inside yourself, identify the areas where you have moved into the '*Bad Habit*' zone, write them down on a piece of paper as and when you can recall them and sit again with your dear ones and elders and ask for their guidance to how to get rid of them one by one. And again make a promise to them holding their hand that you will not back down but face the consequences head–on. Soon you will have a self–realization that you are back to becoming a better person and a better human.

Courage is not a momentary act but a way of life. Let it flow into every aspect of your life. Just reignite it and set it free. It will choose its path henceforth to re emerge in its strongest shape in your life, and this time, do not let it go.

So awaken the child within you and be reborn from the ashes like a Phoenix which does not know about backing out ever. Then 'FEAR' will become '*No Fear*' and when you find yourself again in the very situations that you used to run away from, you will now look at it in the eye and say "*You Are Mine To Win Over*".

VIVID IMAGINATION: THINKING OUT OF THE BOX

When you started understanding the world better, you started exerting your control over the situations you found yourself in by forming a perspective in it that was your own, and not what was prescribed for you by the world.

Say you were handed a piece of clay to make something out of it. Most of you would not only make what was shown in the pictures or told to you but also went beyond it. When you were asked to make a clay car, you not only made a car but also gave it features beyond what you were taught. So for example, for you, the car may have had wings that could make it fly. This was not taught to you but you took the liberty of an artist to let your minds run wild, beyond the scope of what you saw or had been told.

You gave birth to a structure, one that was based on your imagination and was not just the by–product of what was being shown or being taught to you. You became a creator along with being an inventor. Your imagination challenged the boundaries of the thought process you had been familiar with since the beginning, pushing them into unknown realms.

Remember the sketches you drew of your school teachers while sitting on the last bench, that too when the class was in session? It always turned out to be the weirdest and the funniest activity you indulged in during your school days. You drew pointed ears, a long nose, a huge belly and what not. The picture was nowhere even close to how your teacher standing in front of you at the blackboard looked like. Yet this was your way of imagining beyond what was in front of you and directly visible.

If you recall how you participated in '*Science Exhibitions*', you innovated and presented something which was not something you had been learning all your life. You created stuff that you might never even use–stuff that made the audience's jaws drop as they wondered, 'How can this small child design something like this?' And mind you, this was no easy job. But it was possible for you at that age and at that moment because you believed in running your mind wild, you believed in looking for the edge of the world and what's beyond, rather than just accepting what you saw around. Your mind was not confined to the box of the world but went beyond, into spaces beyond your sight and mind.

The idea of presenting a new model for a generator or a motor was something which was not easily conceived. But you made your thoughts go through the twists and turns of ideation and creation to arrive at the final product which you were proud of as it won accolades in the exhibitions. You did not stop at basic, repeated formulae when faced with roadblocks but powered the road–roller of your imagination over the roadblocks and moved ahead to achieve something that was different and new and was enjoyable to create.

When you were asked to draw a house on sheet of paper, every time you drew, the sketch was different from the earlier one, even if the task at hand was same. Your thinking was different every time as your mind kept on exploring further into the vast but unfamiliar and untouched territories every time.

There was no definition of any boundary as such that was accepted by your mind. It took the liberty of wandering into spheres which seemed to be nonexistent to an open eye but a closed mind. Can you recall the time when you broke the egg on the hood of the car to check if it was hot enough to cook the egg? It was out–of–the–box thinking. The result might not have been what you wanted but you still exercised the wildness of your mind.

Whatever situation you faced even in your daily life, it was your street–smart and innovative thinking which defined the actions that enabled you to deal with the situation. Say when you were asked to organize a birthday party with a limited budget, to make the party enjoyable within that limited budget, and you came out with innovative ways to make the party memorable based on your '*Street Smart*' thinking–well, that is nothing but an instance of thinking out of the box. You might not have had the privilege of having an event manager doing it for you. But you still made the party memorable and it was on the lips of every one for the next few days, as people praised your innovative way of organizing the party, right from the food menu, to the games, the decorations, and so on. Go through the snaps of birthday parties you organised and you will soon realise what I mean by creative thinking.

Remember the varied and innovative excuses you made up when caught in situations at home or in school when you were suddenly discovered playing a prank or being naughty? Well take a moment and recall a few of those best excuses and moments.

When you missed completing your homework and when asked for it by your teacher, you probably said that you had completed the home work on time but could not get it to the school as your dog had torn the pages.

Or, when you attempted to pass on a love letter to your love interest but got caught red handed by her/his friends, you made up a story that it was actually a fragment of a script of a play that you both were supposed to act in. See, there is a big smile on your face again! You have suddenly gotten all nostalgic and the words of your first love letter are now dancing in front of your eyes. If you begin to write down the list of excuses you had cooked up while growing up, the list might run into pages. So how did you manage to come up with a new excuse every time to save yourself back in those days? Well, it was nothing but the spirit of imagination in you which had made it possible.

But what have you turned into now? The wild artist, the creator, the inventor, has been put to sleep and the one out in the world has his/her eyes wide open but his/her mind tightly shut. Whatever situation is thrust upon you, you accept it at face value, without trying to look beyond its walls. Your mind has stopped wandering. It thinks about and accepts only what is there in front of it and is projected onto it. You have become a robot repeating the same set of activities day in day out without even exploring what could be beyond the walls enclosing on you.

If there is some work assigned to you, you always follow the conventional steps to complete it. In reality, this is what is pitting you against others in the '*Rat Race*', given that the others also have the same approach wherein you are not confident of your victory — you do not even see the finish line of the rat race as your vision is blocked by the herd of participants running in the race.

You are set in a routine similar to that of a machine which produces the same output, following the same set of activities, day in and day out. Take the example of a PowerPoint presentation you have made over the years. If you recall, you will realise that most of those presentations follow a similar structure, and a similar style and outlook. Now you would say that this forms a part of conventional guidelines. But did you ever experiment, or try changing the look and style before presenting it to the audience. You need to realise that even the audience might be bored by seeing the same type of presentation every time. They too would like to see something different being projected onto them. But you fail to deliver that variety as you too have narrowed your approach and follow the guidebook steps every time.

This also creates a never–ending loop for you where you start losing the confidence of your superiors at work as you do not give them something new when the opportunity strikes at such junctions. This in turn hampers your future career prospects. They realise that you are not someone whom a new project or a new assignment can be handed over to, so you end up doing the same kind of work year on year. And when the time comes for performance evaluation, since you have not really contributed over and above your basic work profile–while your peers are shining as they have extra contributions to highlight — you end up spending years in the same grade and same profile and eventually reach a position where you almost become redundant for the organization and one day suddenly find yourself at the receiving end, being asked to justify your contribution to the organization. This is the final straw — and an indirect signal that the time has come for you to move on and look for career options outside the organization because from having been as asset, you have turned into a liability side for the organization.

Even in your business, you have to always think beyond convention, anticipate the next big change which can disrupt the market, and act on it before the competition does. But as you are stuck in your daily set routine, your mind has stopped operating beyond what you can see others doing. You are unable to gain that extra edge for your business and might lose out to the competition in the long run.

And depending on the nature of your finances, and if happen to have Damocles' sword of EMIs swinging right above your head, you very well know that getting into such a situation might not only ruin your career but the financial hit will break you down on emotional, personal as well as social fronts.

People around you will start avoiding you as they would be scared that you might ask them for financial favours. And once you are cut off from your social circle, your family too suffers a similar fate as they are directly bonded to you.

Your child might have to move out of the school they are going to and shift to a different school as you might be struggling to pay their fees; your spouse, in case he or she is not employed, will now go through the mental pressure of looking for a job and might have to take up something that might ruin their peace of mind and shackle their purpose of existence.

And what about your parents, who were at peace some time ago seeing you settling into your job and taking care of your family but now, with your career in jeopardy, even at their advanced age they have to go through immense mental pressure as all the dreams they had about you come down crashing in one go.

What if you are tagged as an oldie now by your grandchildren as they feel that the bedtime stories you narrate to them are the same old ones which they have already read in school books or in graphic comics? Then they too will start avoiding you more, as one of the most precious memories a child has are the stories narrated by their grandparents. But so long as you remain unable to innovate in your story–telling, they would continue to be deprived of such memories.

You will soon realise that one shortcoming in your life has not only ruined your life but that of your spouse, your children, and your parents as well. They had looked up to you, they idolized you, and they had pinned their hopes for a better life on you–but to no avail. When you get down to playing with your children, you can remember the games you are familiar with and will try to involve them in a similar set of games every time. The child will enjoy it first, but over a period will find it monotonous and boring as its mind is running wild, into innovative spheres. Owing to the exposure they have to what the world has to offer, over a period of time, they start wanting something new.

Think deeper and you will realise that your personal life with your spouse has also become monotonous as you are following the same set of routines, the same set of activities to be with each other in your attempt to preserve your connection with each other. In the beginning, the activities and routine, being new, would bring genuine happiness to both you and your spouse. But over a period of time, it becomes a mechanical and repetitive routine.

You always get to hear '*Think Out Of The Box*'. But even if you give it a thought you will realise that your *Mind–Eyes* cannot look beyond what your conventional eyes can see. You end up leading the life of a rat and continue to run in the never–ending race.

You are so pre–occupied with what is around you that you do not look for the small hole which can give you a vision of possibilities beyond the system you are stuck in. You are also too scared to experiment now as you keep hearing that 'You have grown up' and so follow the set path and lead the life as led by your elders.

In that case, you either accept your fate as a rat running the race all your life, with no sign of the finish line, or you change the rules of the game with your imagination and creativity and emerge victorious in '*The Race*' which matters the most — the race of your life.

We forget that there is a purpose to our life which we have to fulfil — the purpose of changing the world and bringing positive changes, to spread joy and happiness. But today our only purpose seems to be that of survival by any means.

Do you want to lose the race of life and end up being the machine, the robot, having the same life as millions of others like you, or do you want to once again become the innovator, the painter, the artist who has the power to change the game by virtue of thinking out of the box?

When was the last time you learned something new? When did you last try gaining new skills? When was the last time you made your minds run wild, imagining things and situations unheard of? Well lets accept that for most of you, it's been ages, and the reason behind it is the one offered at every instance, 'Don't have time for this'.

Well, if you do not shape your present, thereby shaping your future the way you want it to be, the world will always seem to be a never–ending rat race which will tire you over a period of time, making you a loser and a failure.

The first step is to move out of the dogma of 'Don't have time for this'. See how you can better utilise every second in a day. Can you sleep less? Can you do your daily chores faster? The onus is totally on you how you can fit in spare time to indulge in something new.

If you have a habit of having bed tea, then spend some time reading the newspaper; try multitasking, and read the newspaper while having your tea. Such small changes in your routine might soon generate sufficient extra time that you can allot to learn new skills.

Even if you have a routine that you follow religiously, see how you can manage time better for each of the activities that form your routine. Say you are used to sleeping late at night after watching television for some time to relax after a long day at work. Can you do away with television programs which you just surf through even if you do not really enjoy watching them? Can you do away with that half hour or one hour of indulging in meaningless television–watching and utilise that time for something new?

When you get up in the morning, you will realise that quite often, you tend to have a feeling that you haven't slept enough. So you spend more time lolling in bed even if peaceful sleep is no more to be found. You stay in bed as long as possible.

But the fact is there can be no end to sleep. Once you have got the required quota of sleep to keep yourself fit and mentally charged up, make a promise to yourself that from now on you will not loll around in bed killing more time but immediately get up and channelize that extra time saved into doing something new. In the beginning it will be tough to break the routine you are used to but when you identify what new fun and new activities the extra time can be used for, you will definitely have extra motivation to leave the bed at the first instance of waking up.

The next step is to take up a new hobby—may be learn musical instruments, something you always had a liking for but never took up. A new hobby will get you to break the monotonous routine you are engulfed in and give you an opportunity to express your creative side, thereby not only opening your facial eyes to see something new but also the eyes of your mind to try something new.

Say you always had the creative mind of an artist but could never learn the skills. Well, now is the time to reignite the creative spark lying dormant in you. Check out which art and painting classes are close to your house and office, which of them are suitable to your routine, and join that class immediately. Even if you can take out some time on a daily basis to practice later on, it will keep your mind rolling and bending. And if you are retired and at home, try to learn as many things as possible, and once you are done with one, take up something next, but keep on learning.

The new hobby will reveal things your mind may have never thought it would be able to see, bounded as it has been by high walls that did not allow even a peep into the world beyond. Housewives/househusbands and grandparents tend to spend more time with their children. Well, join your children and grandchildren in their adventures when they take up new hobbies themselves. Being their partner in their hobbies will not only put a smile on their faces but also strengthen the bond between you and the child. Even if you are working, see how you can spare time for being with your children and their hobby activities whenever you are at home or on holidays.

Say your child is learning to play the guitar. You too can take up weekend guitar classes, and when your child is practising in the evening when you are at home, join in. You might also find moments of joy as you discover that here it is your child who is mentoring you as children have higher grasping powers owing to the spirit of a free mind. Your bond with your child will also be strengthened as they will find excitement and fun in reversing the roles and being your mentors this time.

You and your spouse can take up a hobby together, say, join dancing classes or canvas painting classes. This way you will get to spend some quality and fun time together, breaking your monotonous routine, and also will learn something new and creative, With each of you to motivate and support each other, the learning will be quicker and full of happy moments and bring you both even closer to each other.

Next, aim to acquire a new skill set. Say you have never ever cooked in your life. Take it up and make a vow to acquire this new skill and see to it that you walk every step to acquire it. Once you are retired, acquiring such skill sets may surprise and please your spouse.

Say in your profession you are in the field of finance and accounts. Make an attempt to move out from your seats and on to the field. See how customers respond to the pricing set by your logic for a product your organization is offering. From being just a finance resource in your organization, try to look beyond your seat into the marketing angle of it.

In your business, see how you can diversify. Say you have a software development firm, see how you can explore expanding into social marketing and so on where you can run your thoughts towards innovative solutions benefiting your business considerably.

You might have never written an article because there is a separate department which does that in your organization. So even if you have to publish the achievements of your area of work in the internal magazine circulated in your organization, you still ask them to do it for you. Why don't you, this time around, prepare the first draft on your own and then forward it to the concerned department to check and finalise and publish it? For them it will simplify the task as they now would have a ready reference based on which they can finalise the final draft and for you it's an opportunity to let your creativity run wild while gaining a new skill set. There are many more such activities which you can take up to keep on acquiring new skill sets and getting the creative spirit of yours back to work.

Post your retirement, you could take up writing and approach a local newspaper or a magazine firm and offer to write small articles for them based on your experience gained over the years. Or, if you are interested in writing poetry, let your thoughts flow with no boundaries stopping you anymore, and let the creative you out into the open.

If you recall moments from your childhood, you will find that your imagination roamed into unknown territories the most when you ventured into the world of comic books. Tying a towel behind your back and aiming to fly was not the only instance; many of the inventions of the modern world have a root in graphic novels of great imaginary writers of earlier times.

Get back to spending some of your spare time in the world of comic books again as it can push your mind into planes you may have never imagined. Did the thought, "I can't read a comic book now, it's for children and I am a grown up" stream into your mind just now? Well, globally, the adult population is known to be an avid market for comics as they continue the hobby of letting their mind run into planes unknown. So do not let this thought stop you, and if this has been a hobby when you were child, then it will be one of the easiest steps for you to take.

Share the comics with your children, see what they are reading, sit down with them and read them together. You will find a sense of utmost happiness in sharing the moments of fun together. Try to get your hands on different genres of comics — from science fiction to stories of comic heroes and heroines, and so on. By exposing your mind to different styles and different thoughts you will be able to run your own imagination into new territories.

Taking up a new hobby will not only awaken the spirit of the creator and inventor in you but also bring the family closer when such moments of fun and happiness are shared together.

When you begin to climb over the walls of conventional thinking, your mind starts reigniting the spark of an out–of–the–box thinker and you will realise that new avenues are opening up. You will find yourself experimenting to find new and innovative ways of achieving success in your routine tasks, transferring the reins of your life back into your own hands. You will be back as the one in charge of your life and cease being someone who only takes orders.

So awaken the child within you and let your mind wanders into planes never heard of or never tried and transmit your thoughts beyond the box you are in, breaking the barriers which had concealed your thoughts till now.

EXTREME PERSISTENCE: NEVER GIVE UP

When you gained the wheels of your feet and were all set to explore the universe, you fell down, but got up again, fell down, but continued to get up again and again and continued to walk — with the excitement evident from your smiling face — toward your parents and dear ones who were calling out to you.

You were bruised and hurt but you got up and proceeded towards your goal — the open arms of your parents and dear ones.

Before you got your new bicycle, you may have never thought that you could explore the world other than on your feet. But you mounted your bicycle, attempting to pedal ahead, but fell down and quite often hurt yourself. But did you let go off the bicycle? *No*. You went through the crests and troughs of the journey endlessly till you mastered the bicycle.

You derived your motivation from your friends and elders who you saw riding their bicycles happily. So despite your repeated falls, you did not let your desire to learn cycling die down and kept on trying till you learnt it and did not fall ever again.

When you were defeated in a game or match, you went back to the nets, practiced harder, sharpened your skills further, analysed the weakness of your opponents, and came back stronger the next time to ultimately emerge victorious.

You may remember the cricket matches you had played where there used to be some teams you initially were losing all the matches to as they seemed to be stronger because of having better–skilled players — their best batsman was someone you always struggled to get out or their best bowler could exploit a weakness in your armour and get you out soon. But did you give up every time you saw them or were expected to bowl against them or bat against them? Or did you learn from each instance and sharpened your skills to get the better out of you and finally end up hitting their balls out of the park and getting them out in your first over?

Say your weakness had been facing short balls which their best bowler knew about and used to maximum benefit while bowling to you. But you did not let that dent your spirits. You practiced even harder in the nets and over a period gained the required skill to handle such balls with ease, finally emerging victorious against them.

If you are a girl, you can recall the moments when you could see your brother or your male friends learning to ride motorcycles and scooters and roaming around the town. Did you feel at that moment that you are a girl and you can't enjoy in a similar fashion? Or did you walk up to your father or any elder and asked them to teach you also how to ride the motorcycle or scooter?

The vehicle may have seemed heavier to handle initially, and you might have had negative feelings while trying to balance it, and perhaps thought that this is not your cup of tea. But did you give up or did you go ahead with a strong spirit to learn the art of riding the vehicle? You never thought of yourself as inferior to the males, so you never gave up and practiced rigorously to eventually tame the machine.

During the curricular examinations, if you did not understand a given topic, you still went into it again and again till it finally made sense to you. And what about the times when you missed passing some exam or the other? Did you quit schooling, or did you come back the next time and conquer the subject?

And what about the time you fell in love? Did you give up on your hopes the very first time your love interest turned you down? Or did you try again and again to woo the object of your attention? It's true that success was not always a given in this phase of life. But did you restrain yourself from trying any number of times? And it goes without saying that quite a few of you did emerge victorious by winning the admiration and acceptance of your love.

Well, how did this happen, that despite repeated rebuffs, which must have hurt you emotionally and psychologically, and could have made you feel like a failure, you did not stop making your efforts to achieve your goal? Well, it was nothing but the attitude of never giving up — the inbuilt nature of extreme persistence — which turned any defeat into victory eventually.

But as you grew and moved into professional and married lives, this '*Warrior*' took a back seat and a '*Compromiser*' took over. This *Compromiser* always acted from the belief that survival was more important than '*Winning*' –notwithstanding the fact that your heart was broken; your mind had become lame, and your physical self-weaker than ever.

You gave up easily on anything which seemed to be getting you into your discomfort zone. You surrendered yourself to so–called '*Fate*'. You started losing control over your heart, your mind and above all your '*Will*' to succeed. Your life became mechanical and robotic more than ever as your '*Free Will*' was replaced by sets of commands that you were made to follow.

In your work life, if you could not perform, and were not rated well during your performance appraisal, you were demoralised, and rather than improving the next time around, you seemed to be dragging yourself deeper into failure. You took it upon yourself that you are not good enough and are weak when competing against your peers. Hence it was destined from the beginning that you will fail.

When you got married and began to know your spouse better and sharing each other's lives, there were instances where you both might not have been on the same page. But rather than continuing to give each other the required time to understand each other better, you ignored the disagreement the next time around, creating a divide between the two, and started taking your life for granted, thinking of it as your fate and destiny, and as something that is not under your control. This signalled a crack in the shield of happiness that was supposed to bind you both together, as marriage is not an amalgamation of mere life but also of two souls.

When you set up your business, the moment you found that the going is getting harder and it does not seem to be what you had thought of in the beginning, you start giving up and look for justifications–such as that the market is bad, the timing is wrong, and so on, and seek to pull out from it.

As an old person, if you wanted to continue any of your earlier interests but are not good at it anymore, such as, say, playing tennis, you now easily give up when you are not able to match the other players. Very soon you do not want to get onto the court again. You tell yourself that you are getting old, and that you don't have the stamina to continue as before even though you know that it's an activity that helps you keep fit.

Is this what you really want in your life? Do you want to be a command–driven robot all your life? And mind you, what you are and what you do not only impacts your life but also leaves an impression on those around you as your lives are woven together. Man is a social animal, so your actions or not acting directly or indirectly impact those associated with you.

When you were growing up, you looked to your parents as comic book heroes and heroines who could make everything possible. Do you feel that you would be setting up, or are already setting up, a similar vision for your children now? Do you continue to be, or aim to become, the '*Invinicibles*' in their eyes — the ones they will always look up to? Or, in reality, have you let them down by becoming the '*Oppressed*', giving up every time they looked up to you?

Today, when you come home from your job or from your business venture with a frown on your face, do you want your children to emulate this in their lives? Say you had promised to get something for your child on the assumption that you would get a salary revision. But you lost on the salary increment. Will you then go and tell your child that you've lost the spirit to be the best? Or will you promise them that you will work much harder from now on and not give up, and you shall get them more than what they had been promised?

Your parents used to look at you as their reason for pride when you were growing up. Do you feel that by submitting to the challenging situations that come your way today, you can continue to be their reason for pride? When you walk around in the house always in a grumpy mood, will you pass on the right signals to your parents? Will they continue to be relaxed and happy, thinking their child is leading the life in the right track?

As you grow older, if you sit back and start developing a laidback attitude — an absolute transformation from the charged–up individual that you were earlier — your children and grandchildren will start developing an image of you as a person who seems to be giving up on the essence of life rather than someone they can learn from.

Well, the time has come to become the '*Conquerer*', the comic book hero and heroine again in your lives, before it's too late and you are stuck on a point of no return.

First sit down and think about every aspect of your life. Make two columns. In one column, list those aspects of your life where you still feel you have some control. In the other, list those aspects where you believe you have given up and are losing ground. Then choose which moments frustrate you the most and write down everything you can think of in detail. You will soon realise that when you express your frustrations to yourself and not to those around you, you can understand better why you got into this mess in the first place

Many a time you are stuck in situation because you have closed your eyes to it, submitting to it instantly. This process of writing down will help you join the dots from the beginning to the present, helping you identify the path this journey has taken in your life.

Say when you jot down that you have given up excelling in your job or taking your business to the next level and you identify its root cause, it might strike you that you are stuck at the lower grades because you are not taking up the additional responsibility that could help you build an added advantage during your performance evaluation, or that your business is suffering because you are not ready to make the extra efforts persistently to succeed.

Once you realise this, see what you could do to address this. Can you brainstorm and research and come out with an idea, a usage of an innovative technology, to, say, improve customer service? Once you have researched the details adequately, approach your superior and present the idea to them. If your idea is really worthy of the attempt, then your superior may recommend that you take it forward, and once you make it a success, then this additional effort from your side might improve your performance rating the next time around. So, rather than giving up, explore how to make your work more interesting and rewarding.

If you and your spouse have been disagreeing on any point for a long time, and it is hampering the bonding you share, jot it down and identify the root cause and work on it. Say he/she has been wanting to visit his/her relatives for quite some time but every time he/she mentioned it, you refused, saying that you do not have time and are busy at work. When you write it down, and also compare it with why you have been busy and what happens when it comes to you visiting your relatives, it might strike that over the last few months, when it comes to visiting your dear ones, you have already done it more than once but have ignored when it came to visiting his/her relatives as you have been busy. This might be the real reason why he/she was sad and irritated.

So don't give up so easily. Check when is the next possible time that you can take holidays, and if you, say, have a long weekend holiday coming up, decide accordingly and walk up to your spouse and initiate the discussion this time from your side and inform him/her about the plan to visit his/her relatives. He or she would definitely be happy again and your bonding will be rejuvenated.

Next, make up your mind and keep a pledge to yourself that now you will not give in to the situation but give it back with all your might. If you can't take that pledge for yourself, then do it for the ones you love the most — your parents, your spouse, your children, your grandchildren, or your best buddies. Walk up to them and announce your resolution to fight back again and this time with a reignited '*Will*' to succeed.

'*Will Power*' is said to be the biggest reason behind any success. The ones who have strong will power to swim in the most dangerous of tides have the power to change the world, not only for themselves but for others too.

Walk up to your dear ones and discuss with them the issues that had been bothering you, issues where you have been in submissive mode, and discuss with them and decide how you will make the turnaround happen with your efforts and persistence. Then have a conversation with them about each such incident and ask them to keep a close watch on you this time. Keep them posted regularly on the progress of your efforts so that in case you seem to be getting weak again, they can be around to remind you of the pledge you had taken for them.

If you don't like your job or the business you started, then think and understand why you don't like it. Is it because it's from a field you are uncomfortable with due to your own lack of competency or is it because you feel weak comparing yourself with peers who seem to excel in their work? Once you realise what you are lacking in, then go about getting yourself acquainted with that subject by reading about it, or take it upon yourself to learn the required skill set to succeed in it. If possible, join a class where you can learn and acquire the required skill set and give the work at hand another shot.

Say over the years your profile as a computer programmer has moved from *Java* programmer (one of the terms for a specific subject in computer programming) to developing mobile–based applications and you suddenly find yourself in unknown territory, losing the reign of which compels you to a frustrated period in your life. Well, do not give up. Did you know *Java* when you were born? Well, obviously not. But you learnt it over a period of time. So why back out this time when something new has come up? Explore the new avenues again. Learn about it, and if there is still space left to improve, take up a course in mobile–based applications.

In your married life at times you start to take things for granted, assuming that your life is in a total mess and there is no way out. You continue getting frustrated at every instance when you should have been strong but turned out to be the weak link. Well, how many times you have really tried to sit down with your partner and understand why you are in this situation and how all of it started. If you did try this earlier but still the mess exists, it means you went to it with a weak heart that is ready to give up even before getting into the crux of the situation.

This time around, introspect about your inner being and map it with the situations you are in. Then approach your partner with the attitude that this time you will not be the one backing down or running away from solving the puzzle.

Give the confidence to your partner that this time you will not leave the conversation until you have reached a consensus about the way forward. Hear your partner out, strengthen your heart to listen to and accept every remark they make about you, and don't run away from it. Next, present your perspective and outlook on the satiation and propose a solution while asking for more from the partner.

Talk it out thoroughly and when you both are convinced with strong hearts about what you have decided upon, make a promise that you will go all out and give your best this time to make it '*Possible*' and will not be the first one to give up. Once the partners have rekindled the confidence in each other, they might go to great lengths to ensure that this time they do not break the promise, and where there is a '*Will*' there is a '*Way*'. The dawn of a new sun will be around the corner soon, ready to embrace you, and happiness shall return to your faces again.

Remember that with your spouse you do not only share the life but also your soul. So do not let the loser creep in into your life, as for your spouse, you are now the Hero or the Heroine upon whom they have invested their faith and life. So don't give up on any instance and give every situation a fight, such that your objective must be not to survive but to win and conquer.

Your children are always your priority. So now, when you feel they are deviating from the right path towards being a better person, do not lose hope. Keep on trying to talk to them with examples of how they did what was right when they were young, and remind them of those moments and give them confidence by standing with them to make another attempt to make things right.

Every day when you wake up, close your eyes once again, look inside you, listen to the voice of your conscience and remind yourself that no matter how bad the situation is and no matter how bad it will get, you will not give up as you know that these times will pass, that you just have to stand firm in the storm to get what you want as the happy moments are right around the corner. So don't back down now.

So awaken the child within you and reacquire the facet to never give up in any situation ever and keep on punching on the walls till you succeed in breaking it down and achieving what you had set out to in first place, Compromise is for losers and you are not that, so go on and win.

VALUES AND PRINCIPLES – DO AND STAND FOR WHAT IS RIGHT

While you were growing up, you had mentors and guides in the form of your parents and dear ones who helped you imbibe strong values and principles, the pillars which were supposed to support your life through any calamity you were to face over your journey in this world.

Core values and guiding principles like honesty, integrity, and justice were woven into your life. No matter how bad the situation was, how intense the pain was, you never deviated from your beliefs. You stood unmoved, taking the hit bang on yourself but not willing to compromise even an inch on the principles and values your parents and dear ones had passed on to you.

You believed in and practised virtues like honesty, integrity, and justice day in and day out. You were naughty but when faced with the moment of truth, truth was what you sided with. If you played a prank, you also accepted your part in it with full honesty when questioned about it.

Recall the teachings of your parents and grandparents, things such as never lying to anyone. How closely you kept these principles to your heart and never deviated from them! Do you recall the time you kept the tap running in your bathroom to make a fake swimming pool by blocking also the exit drain and played in the water? When your parents found out later that water had run out of the bathroom, rather than lying that you did not do it or that your sibling did it, though you may act innocent initially, you would accept and eventually admit your hand in the naughty prank. It was not that you were scared of your parents or that you were scared of the punishment you might receive if you had hidden your role from them — it was just that your principle would not let you lie to anyone.

You did make excuses, but that was more for the sake of the fun you intended to derive from it. But the moment you realised that the incident was no more fun and was turning into a serious issue, you immediately accepted your mistake.

When you went to a lakeside picnic, your parents instructed you not to get into the deep water and play only on the shore. But your naughty heart pushed you to get into the water and get wet. But when you got back home in wet clothes, you made excuses, saying thing like someone pushed you into the water and that's why you got wet. But when your parents discussed the possible dire consequences of getting into deep waters, you immediately realised the mistake and accepted your part in it and not only that, you also took a vow that you will not repeat such a mistake again.

You stood for what is right no matter how harsh the outcome was for you. You were the first to raise your hand when someone was in need of help. You not only lent your hands to help but also grabbed the hands of others in need and stood by them to sail through the river of tests, aiding them to succeed unscratched.

You not only stood up for your friends but also stood by, in times of genuine need, with those who always seemed to be against you but in this given instance happened to be on the side of what was right and just. For you, doing the right thing was not based on whether someone was your friend but on whether that person was standing for or guarding what is right and is acting in the light of true justice.

Recall the time you got into fights with a particular person in your classroom, someone who always seemed to have a grudge against you. It is very likely that at some point you may have protected or stood by this person only because they were right.

Say when you were made the class representative and were asked by your class teacher to name the children who were playing pranks in their absence. By track record they might automatically also include the ones you may not have good relations with. But rather than taking undue advantage of this situation, if the person was not a part of any commotion created in the class, you would tell your teacher to leave their names out — this was nothing else but an act of justice practiced by you. You would never let any wrong decision prevail if you had a say in the situation, because for you, standing for what is right was greater than any personal benefit you could derive from it.

What about the times when you were made to participate in groups for combined study? Did you chose to share your knowledge with only the few who were in your good books or happened to be your friends, or did you treat everyone in the group as equal? You believed in sharing your knowledge with everyone who was in need, and did not chose the audience — another teaching passed on to you by your elders, which held that knowledge should always be shared and spread because the value of knowledge increases when you share it.

You did not look for short cuts in life but had the courage to abide by your principles and values and followed the path laid for you. You felt a sense of pride whenever you stood up for your values and principles even in testing times. You felt genuine happiness when the outcome was achieved on your terms, in consonance with your core values and principles.

When you were asked to complete an assignment or a task, rather than looking for short cuts and pushing the major work on to others, you participated equally. In case someone did extra work in the group, you made sure you passed on the adequate credit to them accordingly when the evaluation took place. Taking credit for another's work, or taking undue advantage of others' weakness was not something you believed in or practiced or preached.

When you were selected to represent your school team in any sports, say, cricket, if a class mate with whom you did not share a good rapport and who always looked for opportunities to put you down was also a part of the team, you never let the feeling of rivalry take over the spirit of the game. You worked together collectively and gave your best every time so that your school won the trophy.

Remember the time someone from your class was not bright enough and some of the people around made fun of them? You never joined in but always helped them in their studies, made them a part of your friends circle, and never let them feel alienated.

When you found a subject tough to pass, you worked harder on it; you spent days studying late into the night until you understood the topics of the subject you had trouble understanding. You did not indulge in activities such as cheating to pass the exam but believed in the value of integrity which your parents had passed on to you.

For you winning was not everything. But winning based on principles and values was what mattered ultimately to you. Even if you lost but had followed your principles and values, it gave you more satisfaction then winning by unjust means.

But as you grew older and seemed to get more deeply involved in the so called 'harsh realities of life', your thought process changed. The core values and principles you stood for and would bet your life on began slowly to be replaced by the belief that you need to change with times.

But is this change with the times really what makes you genuinely happy, as you once did as a child? Did you ever feel proud again at taking the first step or on going the extra mile? You started to look for short cuts to run away from any situation that put you under pressure with regard to your core values.

Truth and standing up for what is right gave way to how can I benefit from this situation. Your sense of ego and jealousy began to grow stronger than ever. From having been a helping hand, as a child, you were turning into someone who was looking for opportunities to put the other person down at every instance. An interaction with any person was no longer about sharing lives but about outshining them and winning against them at any cost, without even realising that the cost you were ready to pay for massaging your ego were the values and principles your life had been built around in order to survive through any storm.

In your office you always kept your eyes and ears open to plan how you can push your peers down and climb the ladder by stepping on their shoulders. Rather than working together, you were busy looking for opportunities to harm their prospects in front of seniors. Instead of taking the onus of failure upon yourself based on the shortcomings at your end, you got into blame games and tried to prove how inefficient the others were, because of which the outcome of the task at hand suffered.

Say a work was assigned to you with a specific time line; you completed your part and passed it on to the next team member. Now, in case the work began to get delayed, rather than help the other person out so that the work finishes on time, you wait for the time line to get over so that you can show to your seniors that you were more efficient and the work was suffering because of the shortcomings of the other team members.

But is this the team spirit that you practiced and learned when you used to play with other children? In those times everyone was equal in the team but today the concept of team is no longer the same. Today working in a team is simply an opportunity for one to show up the shortcomings of others. The collective essence of a team having given way to selfish individual ego, the team just remained one on paper. What happens in practice is totally different.

In your business, you started looking for unjust means to bag a project rather than improving the USPs of your business. Improving the USP would have helped you in the long term. But you started looking for short cuts in order to rise fast in the industry.

When you were a child, you did not differentiate among genders or family background or status in society, for you every one was equal in your eyes and given due importance. You believed that everyone had right to free will and lead life on their terms. But as an adult, if you are a male and you got married and made your wife an integral part of your life, and she made a huge sacrifice by leaving all her dear ones and came to stay with you and mould your lifestyle. Do you really practice the virtue of equality even now?

When your children got married, rather than supporting your son–in–law or daughter–in–law in settling down comfortably in the new phase of their lives, you always looked for means to put them down and humiliate them to demonstrate who is in command.

As part of group discussions in gatherings, you will try to boast. You will talk about how you have given so much freedom to your wife that she can choose to continue working even after marriage., But when you reach home, rather than helping her in her household chores, which you can, you will instead lie down, or switch on the television, and enjoy even when she is equally or even more tired than you are.

She, even after working the same hours at her work, has to still take care of all the household chores whereas you make a bold statement that you are very tired and want to relax once you are back home and so cannot give her a helping hand.

You and your spouse have stopped living anymore and stopped reaching out to each other. The love binding the two of you together is getting weaker now. You are now pressurised by the same worldly values and social conventions which you had once despised but are now following in order to avoid being labelled as 'outcast' by the society you are part of.

Where did all the talk about equality suddenly vanish? From a person who practiced what he preached, you were changing into someone who only preached but never practiced.

You could not even sense that the short cuts you began taking could only give you short–term gains–gains which can never be sustainable all through your life, and will one day bring you crashing down to earth. You might turn out be a failure in life ultimately — if not in terms of social status and monetary strength, then definitely in terms of having to live with a sense of guilt over what you have turned into.

By practising inequality in the way you treat your son/daughter–in–law; instead of making the life of your children better you started creating a divide between them from the very beginning while also losing respect in their eyes.

If you recall and talk to your parents and guardians, you will realise that among the first seeds they sowed in your conscience was of values and principles. Can you recall that your parents taught you to speak the truth or to be a liar? You very well know the answer.

Can you now look into the eyes of your parents and face them with the same sense of pride when your values and principles are no more yours now?

Can you see that sparkle in their eyes again which twinkled when you were children who followed the path mentored by them?

When you become parents, do you feel you will be able to inculcate in your children the values and principles which are long gone from inside you? Do you really want them to become what you were turning into or you still want them to imbibe the values and principles your parents gave you when you were children? What are or will be your first teachings to your children — to be themselves or someone else, to believe in and fight for justice or to be a coward prospering from the downfall of others?

Rise up to the occasion and change your life before it's too late and the situations go totally out of your control.

The first thing that needs to be done is to get in touch again with your real self, the one which is now wrapped under layers of guilt and wrongdoings. Recall and remember the core values and principles you once had in your heart. Remember the moments when even through the hardships, they were always your guiding light and got you success and happiness.

You feel that you have changed as you have to change with the changing times. But are these changes really worth what you have achieved? Listen to your heart and try to realise: Do you still have the peace of mind and the sense of genuine satisfaction which you achieved when fighting the war of life with the mace of your values and principles? And once the answer strikes you, promise yourself that you will become that real '*You*' again, the *You* that had been lost over time. Believe in yourself again and believe in the strength of your values and principles. Go back to your parents, your children, your grandchildren, and your spouse and your dear ones, and tell them that now you have resolved to stand for what started your journey in the first place. Once you have committed to the ones you cannot afford to lose from your life, the hard part is over and now is the test which will decide whether you really loved them and will do everything for them.

List down the situations you are facing currently where you have compromised on values for short–term gains and go and take them head–on now. If you have taken short–cuts at work to succeed at the cost of others, get back to your superiors and tell them the truth with a token of genuine apology. It might happen that they might take strong action against you, and this might adversely impact your career in the short–term. But it may also happen that they appreciate your courage in coming clean and accepting your mistakes. And do not forget to apologise to the one on whose shoulders you stepped to ride up the corporate ladder. Whatever be the outcome, you will find the peace which had long been gone from your life.

If you have bagged a deal on unjust methods, approach your client and open up. You need not take anyone's name or blame anyone but you can clear your stand. You might lose the deal immediately. But on the other hand, it might also happen that they support your stand and are happy to see that finally someone had the guts to follow the right path. Even if you lose the deal, there is a higher probability that you might win a business deal with the same company in the future as now they know that you will be taking the right path and would give everything to complete the task in the best way.

If you have not been able to keep up with the expectations of your spouse, your parents, your dear ones and your children and grandchildren and have been lying every now and then to create an impression that you are in command of your life, you are setting up a disaster waiting to happen. This is because in reality you are drifting away from them with each lie that you say. Once the truth comes out, as it is bound to, you will find your world crashing down in front of your very own eyes. List down these situations too, walk up to your dear ones with a clear heart, look into their eyes, hold their hands, spell out your mistakes, and apologise for what you have done, while promising that with the lies now out in the open, you are going to give your best shot to repair the damage which was done.

Communication or the lack of it is the reason for every success or failure in life and if communication is crystal clear, then any failure will turn to success now or later.

Whatever be the outcome, you will soon realise that it was worth the shot as peace returns to your heart through the small hole of '*Hope*' riding the escalator of values and principles.

You will feel happy and satisfied that you have finally found the '*Real You*'. Next, take an oath that whatever situation you are in, you will face it with the strength of your values, that you will face the situations of life as the '*Real You*' and not the compromised version of you. So for instance, try not to jump the traffic signal the next time and wait for the signal to turn green. Do not throw litter on the streets and wait till you reach a place where there is a dustbin. These may be small steps but they will propel you towards bringing about the hoped change.

Initially you will face hurdles and temporary failures. But don't back down now as half of the distance in the journey of transformation had already been traversed when you showed the courage to come clean with your dear ones. You will soon realise that nothing matters in this world more than you being the reason for a genuine smile on their faces.

This time around, don't sit back and crib about issues which directly or indirectly impact your life. You do have a role to play. So for example, go out and vote the next time when elections are held in your town. Participate in the weekly or monthly meetings of your housing society, raise the issues that you have always been cribbing about, and figure out ways to sort them out. Similarly, participate in resolving the issues raised by others as well. Actively participate in all the activities that you can to help bring about positive change in society, in your locality, and in your life.

Lend a helping hand to people around you whenever you find yourself in such a situation. Say the next time when you witness an accident on the road, do not just be a '*Watcher*' but be a 'DOER' and immediately plunge into getting the person the necessary medical attention, etc. You never know when your standing up for what is '*Right*' might be the reason for someone to be alive. So be a good citizen not only of the country but also of humanity. Won't you expect help when in a similar situation? So if you do, then you should also extend your helping hand when it's needed.

So awaken the child within you and become the '*Real You*' that gets your dear ones' heart beating with pride.

A DREAMER–FOLLOW YOUR HEART

When you were growing up, you had dreams of becoming '*That*' and '*This*', of doing '*It*' and reaching '*There*' from '*Here*', and so on. At one moment, you were your normal, present self and in the next, you were running about in your house pretending to be a glimpse of your future. You may have heard your parents shouting, 'Have you gone crazy?' Well, this sense of craziness was the stepping stone to the dreams you began having for your future self. The journey from '*Now*' to '*Then*' had begun even at this early age.

As a child, there was no end to dreaming. You wanted to join the armed forces and serve your country, you wanted to become a sports person representing your country globally, you wanted to become a movie star with a huge fan following and live the life of a celebrity, you wanted to become a top notch businessman, and much more, not to mention dreams of making 'n' number of trips to other planets as an astronaut. This was your dream of becoming your future self, and this was the dream of finding fun and happiness in every moment of your life.

Close your eyes again and recall what dreams you had when you were growing up. Did you dream to becoming an astronaut, an engineer, a doctor, or a movie star? Whatever your dream, at that age, it was backed by your determination to make it come true.

Though the reality is that it's tough to have so many avatars in one life, while others may have seemed plainly impossible, you never stopped dreaming. And when you zeroed down on what you wanted the most, you went all out to achieve it.

Say you chose to become an engineer. You then started taking steps towards that goal by taking an avid interest in subjects which would be the stepping stone for the career of an engineer. You took up extra classes to get in–depth knowledge of the concerned subjects and started spending more time on gaining required exposure to the topics relevant to that field.

Most of your dreams were termed crazy by your parents and dear ones, as it broke the conventional route expected from you owing to the system and society you were a part of. But did you really back out on and stopped dreaming and decide to shift to a conventional life, or did you say to yourself, '*It's My Dream And I Am Its Guardian And I Will Protect It From Dying*'.

You might have had a dream of, say, becoming a journalist. This must have seemed an unconventional carrier choice at that point of time. Your parents may have found it hard to understand and pushed you towards more conventional choices such as engineering or medicine. But did you back out immediately or did you start acquiring knowledge in your chosen field? You might have started taking small steps, such as sending your entries to be published in the children's section of your local newspaper and so on, to start gaining an exposure in that field.

When you were out there in the scorching sun playing a game of cricket or soccer, passers-by would say that the children have gone crazy as they are standing in the sun. But you ignored those remarks as deep down you knew that that is what you enjoyed the most — being out there on the field, sweating it out — it was the sign of the passion that drove you to explore territories beyond the conventional.

You were out there in sun as you dreamed of becoming the next sensation in the game of cricket or soccer.

Girls might be able to recall that when they were growing up, they, too, may have had dreams, say, of becoming a Civil Engineer. But they might have been discouraged by elders telling them that they are girls and their future is to be a housewife taking care of their spouse and their children, and that they have to ultimately lead their entire life in the shadow of their spouse. Similarly Boys might have dreams while growing up of say becoming a Dancer, but they too might have been discouraged by elders telling them dancing and singing suit the girls and not the boys as they are to grow up into men taking the reign of family in their hands. But did any of you let go your dreams or did you walk up to your parents, speak your heart out, and express your zeal to achieve your dreams? You then started taking small steps toward it, such as opting for science stream in your senior years at school, participating with a solo dance item in cultural events at school and so on.

A dream is when you break away from the set path and look to chart a new path for yourself. This required thinking beyond what you were taught or had seen; this required doing things which were not handed over to you by your dear ones. This required the challenging of the very notion of '*Be Like Him*' that may have been thrust upon you by your dear ones.

Did you really want to become like someone else or did you want to lead life on your own terms and achieve what was unconventional and what you had dreamed of always? You more often than not chose to become '*You*' and took up the task of charting new paths for yourself. And when you took the first step toward realms unknown, your act of defiance was termed '*Crazy*' only because you were doing something that had not been taught to you. Besides, your heart was totally into it, and the spirit to succeed was at highest level, which is again a symptom of so–called craziness. Do you recall the time you were asked to become an engineer because your father was one or because your cousin or elder brother was one? But when you spelt your heart out and laid out your dreams in front of your dear ones, say, to become a professional photographer, most of the time, the first reaction from your dear ones was to discourage you. They tried to show you how comfortable the life of an engineer is because you can get a job immediately after your education and can start being financially independent whereas the amount of struggle in a career like that of a photographer is immense. But did you let go of your dreams, or did you set your heart on doing everything you could to make your dream come true? Did you choose to join the herd or to make a separate identity for yourself?

The mind operates through your eyes and ears. It gets easily influenced by external factors. And so the decisions taken by you are often situational and system–driven and many a time, you may end up deciding in favour of what you never truly wanted but chose anyway owing to the pressures created by the system and the ease of relying on what you see and hear.

Listening to your heart, on the other hand, does not depend solely on what you hear or can see but what you can feel inside yourself. The conscience talks to you and sends signals guiding your decisions. When you listen to your heart, the outcome becomes less relevant and what matters is the feeling of being empowered to listen to your inner conscience which knows you the best.

But as you grew older, the spirit of craziness is taken over by the sadness of joining the '*Herd*'.

Rather than becoming the '*You*' you had set your heart on becoming in the first place, you became a part of the '*Herd*' where your identity seemed to have dissolved completely in the crowd.

Dreams get replaced by desires. Rather than dreaming to be someone you always wanted to be, or doing what you always wanted to do while journeying through the sea of happiness and joy, the desire to achieve the end result began to acquire prime importance — and this end was not about living the dream but surviving in life.

You started giving excuses that you have grown up and have responsibilities. So, rather than following your dreams, listening to your inner voice, and being crazy, you decided that it was time for you to join the crowd and lead a normal life. But did you ever check with your heart if this was what you really wanted?

Was this what you had stood up for all these years, and will you let the castle of your dreams disintegrate and fade away so soon?

The dream of a photographer, which seemed to be on track until a few years ago, was derailed over a period of time. What you chose was to follow the same safe path of getting your higher education in the most common of streams, and taking up a job in the most common of fields as you felt that you wanted to lead a normal life and had lost the spirit of a crazy dreamer.

When was the last time you heard people say that you are crazy? When was the last time you did something which was your dream and not something that other people wanted you to do? As a child, you used to love running around in the rain. When was the last time you enjoyed getting soaked in the rain? Your first probable reaction is to say that this is crazy. Don't say that you stopped getting wet in the rain because you did not want to fall ill. Have you really become that much weaker while growing up? Don't say that your clothes will get wet or get dirty, because they can be cleaned again. Stop giving excuses to yourself as your inner conscience knows you better than your mind.

When was the last time you tried doing something new, something which you were not taught or guided to do? Don't say that you don't have the time for all of this. Well, this is your life ultimately, and if you can't live for yourself, you will never be able to have the required level of dedication to live for others as your own self has already become weak.

As a kid, when you were told you were acting crazy, you never felt sad about it and ignored it most of the time and felt a sense of pride in attempting to achieve what you dreamt of. But now you have become so bothered with what people might say about you and what image you have carved for yourself in society that you are scared to be alienated from groups you have become associated to.

You do not want to be left out of the crowd even if the price to be paid is your own dream which, as a child, you had vowed to protect. Was it really worth letting go of your most cherished dream, a dream that you did everything to achieve as a kid?

You might have taken up the family business but was it really what you wanted? Or you might have started a business but in a segment which seemed to be safe rather than something which you dreamed of doing, say you got into online marketing rather than starting a restaurant as you'd always wanted to do.

You might have dreamed of taking up new adventures once you grew old and had retired from your job and had lots of free time. But now, when that time has finally come, you feel that you are too old or too weak to follow your heart.

When you dream, over a period of time, people around you tie their '*Hopes*' to you. Can you walk up to your parents and dear ones and tell them that you failed to live for yourself and your dreams? What will you teach your children — that they should stop dreaming one day, that they must let go of their dreams completely as you did? Or will you teach them to take control of their lives and dreams and never let go?

Do you feel that your parents will be happy and proud of you now that you are living the life of machine, a shadow of your true self, having crushed all your dreams and become a part of herd? When you were growing they might have lauded you and praised you in their circle saying what a great photographer you are and how proud they were about seeing you living your dreams. But when they see the photographer lost in time, do you think they experience the same sense of pride, or are they depressed by the fact that you chose to bow down to the pressure of society and killed your dreams? You in a way have stopped breathing; you are just inhaling the air to somehow survive in this world; you are no more the real '*You*'; you are now one among the many; you are one of a group and no more '*You*'; you don't have your own face; you are recognized by the face of the group you are part of and not by who you are as an individual.

Do you want to live all your life like this and get lost in the sands of time and one day be wiped out of the memory of those around you? Don't you want to create a separate identity for yourself? Don't you still want to inspire the generations to come, and be known as the one who lived by his/her dreams and changed the world because he/she saw the world from their own eyes and not from the eyes of the herd he/she was pushed to be a part of?

An individual's identity is formed or projected to the world only when he or she is able to express himself/herself from their heart, and this happens only when one does that which the heart approves.

A singer expresses himself/herself through the art of singing. Similarly, a chef expresses himself/herself through cooking, and a player through the sports they play, and each of them creates a separate identity of him/her through this act which comes by following his/her heart, and this is an identity which separates him/her from the herd their peers have been following. Do you still have that mode of self–expression alive within yourself, bringing out which will help create your own identity, separate from that of the herd? For only in this will you not only excel but also become a role model for others. Since there are very few who can follow their heart, the world looks up to them for inspiration as they are not part of the herd but a separate being.

Well, all is not lost still. You might not become the astronaut you always wanted to become. But when you dig deep inside yourself, you will find many more dreams which have been locked away in the dark corners of your heart. Unlock them now and vow to live out a few moments of craziness again.

Go out and soak in the rain if you loved it as a child. And if you are a parent or grandparent, do it with your kids or grandkids. It will strengthen your bond with your child if you join them in their dreams and moments of craziness by becoming a child again. Take your dear ones on an unplanned trip. Move out of your comfort zones and march into new unplanned territories.

If you love to eat, wake up in the morning and decide to try a new dish that day. Cook something new by experimenting safely, with the basic food ingredients mixed into the dish this time. Walk into a restaurant and order something which you have never tried before, preferably something whose name sounds weird even to say aloud, and see how there could be a few moments when the craze can be crazier than before.

Utilize your retirement fund, and once every few months book your tickets of a new place you have never been to and take your spouse along.

'*Passion*' gallops on the chariots of '*Craze*' and '*Dreams*'. So if you are passionate about something, craze will creep in to let you live the dream.

Dream not to be somebody but to do something to change the world around you for good, and you will become that somebody anyway once you go through the journey of doing that something.

Make a list of childhood dreams and identify the one that you can still achieve with a little perseverance. Say you always loved dancing and wanted to become a professional dancer one day. Go back to the basics, set aside some spare time, and join a dance class. Those around you, including your family, might say that you have gone '*Crazy*' as you are not in the right age category to do all this. But don't back out as this refusal to back down is what had kept the ball rolling in the first place when you dreamed as a child.

With extreme perseverance, you might become a professional dancer. But even if you do not, you will soon realize that you have met the real '*You*' again and will cherish the act of defiance with a smile on your face and a sense of satisfaction that you were attempting to re–live your dreams.

What about the profession you dreamed of pursuing as a child before opting to become a software developer, or something else totally different from your dream? You might not be able to, say, join the air force now as you have already crossed the age limit, but your next dream of becoming a professional photographer is still possible. You can take it up as a hobby now and start sharing your photographs online and see if you can attract people to like your work. Build on the attention you receive and organize an exhibition of your photographs. This might not turn you overnight into a professional photographer, but it will give you a sense of satisfaction that you are living your dreams and working towards making them real. Where there is a '*Will*' there is a '*Way*' to make your path and live your dreams.

Next, talk to your grandchildren, children or siblings, your spouse, your parents and your dear ones and help them open up about their dreams even if it sounds the craziest thing ever. Try to understand how you can assist them in achieving their dreams. Be the dreamer again but not only for yourself but also for the ones you care for as their craze might rub off on your passion for your dreams too when you guide them on the path of their dreams.

Have you ever asked your parents or spouse about their dreams? They have long lived on dreams for you. The time has come for you to let them live out their dreams now. Say your mother or spouse always wanted to become a singer but owing to societal and family pressure could not take it up. Sign her up this time for a singing class and try to accompany her to the classes every now and then.

Society and the people around might call her crazy, as they are used to seeing her differently. But when they look around, sooner or later they will realize that the world had already moved in that direction, and it's just that your mother has finally started living her own dreams–dreams that she had sacrificed for a long time in order to let you live your dreams. This craze will not be easy to come and be accepted in her age but you have to impart confidence to your mother that living her dreams and being crazy is her '*Right*' and no one can take away her happiness and her dreams from her any more, irrespective of how the people around her may react.

Join your children and grandchildren in giving birth to their dreams and support them till the time they can take their dreams ahead on their own. The crazier they sound, the happier you should feel, as you need to realize that now they are treading the path of their dreams, which they will be passionate about, and which will give them utmost pleasure and happiness. When they come to you with a notion of their dream, do not turn them away, terming it crazy, but join them and embark on the crazy ride with them.

This time with your children and grandchildren play with the butterflies together. Make paper planes and swing together into the sky above. Make paper boats and float them in the river together. Stay up late in the night together hogging the last bite of cake in the refrigerator even if you have office in the morning. Be the dreamer and let others live their dreams too.

Your spouse too might have been sacrificing his/her dreams to make the journey together with you more comfortable. See how you can help him/her achieve those of his/her dreams which he/she still can. Say your wife had always wanted to learn mural painting and landscape–sketching. Then get her to join classes to learn the same and encourage her every day to spend some time practicing it. Say your husband always loved to play video games, buy him a new console from your savings or retirement fund on his next birthday as a surprise gift and play it jointly to see him smiling and enjoying it.

Dreams may be small or big — it does not matter much provided it brings the utmost happiness to your heart. So awaken the child within you and become the '*Dreamer*' who is ready to drive through the bends of life with a renewed passion to live out his/her dreams.

HUMANITY: WILLINGNESS TO SHARE AND THE VALUE MORAL OF EQUALITY

Do you remember when as a child you found a bird in your yard or garden, hurt and bleeding? Well, do you recall what did you do with it? Did you leave it there to die, or did you pick it up or called your parents to pick it up? You got it into your house, fed it, gave it water to sip, bandaged it and once fit again, let it to fly away to its freedom.

Do you recall how many times you had brought a puppy home when you found it being chased by older dogs, and then handed them over to a dog shelter? When a cow in your vicinity gave birth to its calf, you ran to see it every day after your school and played with it. What was it that made you have emotions for animals? Well, this was among the first signs of the birth of humanity in you.

When your pencils became short and your parents bought you a new one, rather than throwing it away, you gave it to the children of your domestic help so that they can use it in their schools. Every year when you bought new school uniforms and new books, your old ones were passed on to the under–privileged and you felt a sense of joy in giving away even your most prized possessions to the needy. You did not indulge in charging second–hand prices for the books or the clothes as this was not a business for a you but an act of sharing happiness.

When you learned to ride your bicycle, you also taught it to the children of your domestic help who did not have a bicycle to learn on, and you shared your toys with them, and also the collection of comics you had with you.

When you got similar gifts on your birthday and could not use all of them at the same time, you passed on a few of them to your other friends. Say you got three chess boards, then you kept one with you and passed on the remaining two to your friends who did not have one.

Did you choose friends on the basis of caste or creed or the family status or everyone who touched your heart became your friend, enjoying the same attention as anyone else in your circle?

Can you pause now and recall the names and faces and background of all of those who were part of your group when you were very young? You will realize that a few of them were not from the same financial or social background as yours but you regarded them as equal to everyone else in your circle.

You believed and practiced the unwritten law of equality passed on to you by your parents and guardians through their teachings.

When it was a festival or a special occasion and you were asked by your parents to take blessings from elders, you took the blessings from your domestic help or driver too as they also held the similar post of a guardian and an elder in your eyes.

Your birthday party invitees were everyone and your friends included the children of your domestic help as well, as they were also a part of your friends circle.

When you went out with friends, you never hesitated to chip in extra on the bill for ice–creams or burgers, accommodating for the ones who could not pay owing to their financial constraints. Similarly, when a new cricket bat or ball was to be bought, only the ones who had financial privilege contributed but the bat or ball was equally used by each and every member of the team irrespective of whether they could financially contribute or not.

Come the time of festivals, you went to the houses of friends and relatives for their blessing. You went to every one's house, including that of your domestic help, your driver, or your not–so–privileged friends, and you all sat on the same floor together and had the same food in the same serving plates that they had in their houses, and relished it with the same fervour as you did in your own house.

You used to teach the younger children of the less privileged what you had learned in your school as they did not have similar schooling exposures. You took time out to help them with their homework, also providing additional exposure to the same subject through your learning. Say you were being educated in an English–medium school but these kids went to Hindi–medium schools, you used to teach them English along with their normal curriculums.

Your domestic help, driver, etc. were not addressed by the name of their function — as 'Maid' or 'Driver'–but as Uncle, Aunty, Big Brother or Elder Sister, owing to the respect they held in your hearts and lives.

You would enjoy a marriage in the family of the less privileged with the same gusto as you would a marriage in your own family even if the pomp and show at their event was lesser than what you enjoyed at your own family's wedding functions. You did not mind extending your helping hand to help make the arrangements, and ensured that the function was held successfully as you realized the importance of that special day in the lives of everyone involved.

A share of your pocket money or money which you got on occasions like birthday, festivals etc. from your elders always went to spending it together with your friends, including the ones who did not have the benefit of having similar monetary support.

When you were asked about your dreams, it was first about changing the world, and adding to the betterment of society, your friends, and your country. The concept of '*Humanity*' took charge of all your dreams and aspirations. If you wanted to join the army, it was to serve the nation. If you wanted to become a scientist, it was for the betterment of human civilization. If you wanted to become a singer, it was to please people through your songs and touch their hearts. If you wanted to become a sports person, it was to bring glory to your country. Money or status in society was lower in the strata of what motivated you to do what you wanted to do.

As you wanted to become a better person, even the money you could accumulate through your profession you wanted to use to help the needy. You wanted to continue to inspire the next generations to allow the feeling of humanity to continue growing stronger in their hearts.

But as you grew older, '*Humanity*' was slowly getting replaced by '*Monetary*'; you became heavily driven to perform activities which could get you more money. '*Doing Good*' was replaced by '*Earning Good*' and the feeling of being a part of the world was eroded, bringing out a new '*You*' which wanted to be more self–centered.

You started looking for opportunities to exploit the weaknesses of others at work. Say if someone did not have a good command over conversing in English, then rather than seeing how you can help them gain the required fluency, you mocked their English during team gatherings, or de–motivating them so that they got depressed and moved out from competing against you during performance appraisals. That way, the next promotion might automatically come to you.

You gradually started to distance yourself from the less privileged, and your circle included only the ones who seemed be on similar or stronger financial status, and having similar or better backgrounds. You continued keeping in regular touch with the privileged ones and started drifting away from the less privileged even though during your childhood years they had the same importance in your lives as everyone else in your circle.

You lost touch with the less privileged friends and modified your basic principle of making friends. You started moving exclusively into the spectrum of people who you would like to be seen or known with rather than the ones who primarily touched your hearts.

You stopped going out with the less privileged friends, stopped contributing to the pool as you used to earlier when you ate or went out sight–seeing because you feel you are now short of money and the world has progressed to become a costlier place to survive now. Slowly, you began omitting the less privileged from joining you in your get–togethers and you went ahead and increased the divide of inequality further.

Your birthday party invitee list was now carefully chosen by you, and you made sure that only those who can contribute towards your success were part of it. The ones left out should not even be aware that you are throwing a party to celebrate your birthday. Hence you made sure to ask your invitees not to mention their invitation to those you had not invited.

Friends that you could not live without seeing every single day you stopped meeting or talking to for days on end even though you had technological advancements such as cell phones to bring you closer. Once upon a time the mere sight of them would bring a smile on your face. But today even a rare call from them aroused the suspicion that the call is for some personal favour that they require from you. You wonder with a frown, 'Why are they calling me'? Your first reaction is to ignore the call or to cut the call short, saying that you are busy. You did not feel guilty enough about it to call back later, never mind that the call might have been a genuine act of friendship where your friend only wanted to know how you had been doing, or merely an invitation to a celebration of their happy moments.

But let someone from your existing or aspiring circle call you at that instance. Not only will you accept the call with a smile on your face, you will also have all the time in the world to listen to that person. And you would somehow take time out from your busy schedule to participate in any gathering they proposed.

If you were invited to, say, the marriage of your childhood friend–someone who is no more a part of your core circle now — you will suddenly find yourselves caught up in too much work to be able to attend the event, even though it might be within city limits and the family is well–known to you. But an invitation from your current or aspiring circle will prompt you to travel the distance of even a few thousand miles even if almost the entire family concerned is unknown to you.

For you, choosing how and where you spend your time is motivated by the short–term or long–term, direct or indirect monetary/non–monetary benefit that could accrue to you from your association with the individuals in question. The joy in your heart is replaced by a concern about how heavy your pocket could become, with no regard for how much emptier your heart was becoming.

When you used to meet your less privileged friends out in the market or at a common friend's place, you were thrilled to see them and were excited to spend time with them. But now, if you suddenly ran into those friends, you will immediately seek an escape route from their company, with the most common answer being, '*I Am Busy So I Will Meet You Later*'.

You loved to catch a ride on their bicycle during your childhood days but when you meet them on the road now, you will hesitate to offer them a lift back home even if you were going in the same direction as you now want to avoid being seen with them in public.

Your senior citizen clubs now only include people from a similar financial and social status as you would like to continue the lifestyle that you had when you were working.

When was the last time you went out of your way to help a less privileged person or spent time with them?, You are now so obsessed with your ego and self–image that you will not attempt anything that might '*Tarnish*' your image and your status in society.

As a child, you occasionally visited old age homes and orphanages to share your little joys with them. But now it's been ages since you stepped foot in such places.

Is this really what brings pleasure to you? Is this really setting the right examples for your children and young ones? Do you even realize what your guardians and parents might be going through when they see their teachings being shredded into pieces by you? Is your position in society and your financial strength all that defines how you should be seen, or is the aspiration of your guardians — of turning you into great human being — worth a shot?

Did all their teachings go in vain? When they wanted you to have genuine moments of joy based on your choices and not on the basis of the choices pushed on to you by the society and system–was it an exercise in futility? Is being rich more important than being happy? Can't you still have a balance between the two? Do you want your children to look at the world from unequal eyes? If you realize that today more and more parents are being made to stay away by their own children, do you want to suffer the same fate through the hands of your child when they turn your age? You have not stepped foot in an old age home for years. Do you want to someday find yourself in one when you fade into the sunset of life?

This is likely to happen as inequality and inhumanity creeps in, and slowly builds up to engulf every relationship — even those that have a bonding of blood. That's because your mind has taken total control of your life and softer emotions have no chance of surviving. From being a human, you have morphed into a machine, operating solely on the input–productive output model, with all empathy lost in the winds of change.

When you find yourself at the end point of your life, do you want to be all alone, with only a few around you, that too consisting only of those who are there only because they are deriving a direct or indirect monetary benefit from being associated with you, or do you want to go out with the same love and care that was there in abundance when you were welcomed into this world?

A winner has a short stay at the top and it exists even shorter in the memory of the people around when they stand alone in the victory lane. But they can inspire generations when they have their dear ones welcoming them at the winner's pit, which is only possible when the winner is a '*Human*' and not a '*Machine*'. Machines can generate awe but not inspire generations, for the latter is only possible for a '*Human*'.

Do your peers and seniors at work address you as Engineer, or System Tester or do they address you by your name, or as sir/madam? You know the answer. But when it comes to your home, you address your domestic help as 'Maid', your driver as 'Driver', and so on. Are you a different species from the ones working for you, or is that you have come from a different planet that you should be addressed differently? Is it not the case that they too are employed in a job the same way as you are employed by others? Then why do you call them by names based on their profession and can't give them the respect they deserve?

Well, give yourself one more chance to be '*Human*' again, to be someone whose heart stops and beats again at the sight of your dear ones and not the ones who exist solely for the purpose of non–emotional benefits.

Make a list of the all the closest buddies and dear ones you had while you were growing up, ascertain their latest whereabouts using the power of social media if necessary, and once the details are at hand, contact them and visit them again. Remind them of how close you were as kids, and though time may have moved you apart, tell them that you still wish to revive the bond of friendship, and that you look forward to being together again. Then stick to the promise you are making.

Go and meet their spouses and their children with your family, and see how your spouse and children can gel with them the way you two bonded once long ago. Exchange stories about how strong your friendship was during your growing–up years, how much fun you two had playing pranks, how much you both learned from each other, how supportive you were of each other, and how strong your bonding was.

Respect the elders again irrespective of their association with you. Your old driver, who used to be 'Uncle', would have turned into '*Driver*' by now. Re–invent your thoughts and get back to respecting him as 'Uncle' again. Do this with everyone who has had a positive impact on you while you were growing up.

Do not differentiate between your grandchildren and the children of your domestic help. If you buy a chocolate for your grandchildren, teach them to share it with the children of your house help as well.

See if you can teach the children of the house help subjects which you had a command of. Buy occasionally a gift for your house–help, driver and other supporting hands — not necessarily something very expensive but something which might be really helpful to them. Thank them in front of your family members and hand over the gift. This will really create moments of genuine happiness for them as they would get the feeling that their hard work has finally been recognized by the people around.

Whenever you order food from outside, or there is something special getting cooked, ensure that a portion of that is also shared with your house–help, drivers, and other supporting hands. This will help you bridge the gap of inequality created earlier either knowingly or unknowingly.

Check about your house–help's children and see if you can help them get a better education, because '*Good Will*' should always start from home. Then take it upon yourself to make sure that they get it.

Vow to invest time and money in some charitable activity. To start with, at least once a month, visit an old age home or an orphanage and bring joy to their inmates with your visits. This might not turn you into a big scale philanthropist but it can restart the '*Human*' touch point in your heart again.

Take at least one less privileged child under your wings and groom him/her in the area of your expertise (assuming it's to their liking). Whether it's your strength in your career, say, information technology, or your area of personal interest, say, your skills as a guitarist, you can take out some time and guide the child in that field. You will soon realize that not only are you helping the child achieve its dream but you are also connecting to your own true self more often. Such an act of nurturing another human being could create a great sense of joy and achievement in life. The next time you get any invitation from a less privileged acquaintance, make an effort to be a part of their happy moments. Don't just be a passive observer of the occasion but also see how you can lend a helping hand toward arranging the function in the best possible way. Reach there a day earlier and see if you can help in setting everything up. See if you can stay on for a day or so and ensure that the function is wrapped up smoothly.

Lead by example and stand out as a role model for your children and dear ones so that you can touch their hearts and help them continue to be '*Human*'. It's your duty now that you do not let them slip into the vicious hole which turns '*Humans*' into '*Machines*'.

The next time you see an accident on the road, do not drive away. Stop and see how you can help the one in distress. Such small steps will propel you towards bringing about the change hoped for.

So awaken the child within you and become the '*Human*' again, believing in humanity above all, You will then soon realize that you no longer have to make an effort and it has turned into a way of life that gives you immense pleasure–pleasure that's sweeter than what any victory or success can bring.

THE CHILD IS BACK

Life goes through many turns, but if you have the control of the steering wheel in your hands, you will be able to make the turns at your will instead of being driven by some other self. A child is least influenced by the system. It can see through the limitations of it.

Not very long ago you had the spark in your eyes, a genuine smile on your face, and the conviction in your heart to change the world. But the dreamer had been put to sleep by the toxins in the environment created by the system. Let's drink the tonic of change and awaken again the child who will spread joy and happiness and be the agent of change for yourself and the dear ones around you. Even if you can recreate the spark in your heart and guide your life towards the purpose of your existence in this world, you would have done enough justice to why you came into the world in the first place.

Either get back into the '*Rat Race*', where you aim to own the track, or you change and explore tracks that you have not explored before. Touch as many lives and as many hearts again as you used to as a child and contribute your part towards bringing about change in the world.

Don the '*Hat*' of explorer again, run your mind into territories unknown, be fearless in your approach, think the unthinkable, never give up, abide by your values and principles, live to realize your dreams, and strive to make a selfless contribution to humanity.

Life does sometimes give second chances to correct what's wrong, to achieve what's left in the dreams basket, to create an identity for oneself, to become a role model, to leave your legacy, and to finally to fulfil the purpose of life. So do not lose hope and try again to win that second chance from life.

From chaos emerges pattern — the pattern of peace and happiness–but for that you must be ready to begin the journey of change that your life needs now more than ever. You must reorient yourself for the stage in life where happiness and joy will be all around you. So don't give up now. As a child, you made the efforts that has brought you this far. Now capitalise on the start you had as a child and build your life in your own way.

You can still be a Hero or Heroine by doing simple things like paying your taxes on time, by helping the needy, by standing up for what is right, by touching as many lives as you can, inspiring others to follow your path, and above all by attempting to spread joy and happiness in whatever you do.

When you were a child, you wiped out what was written on the slate and wrote something new on it again. Give the same chance to yourself, to learn something new again. If you feel that you are too full to learn something new, introspect, and let go of those aspects of your life that are not permitting your life to move in a new direction. Fill the jar of life again with a fresh perspective on life.

Make a genuine effort to not only awaken the child in you but touch every heart around you whose child is still asleep. Help awaken it so that it breaks the shackles of lost purpose. Help such people rework the purpose of their existence on this earth and lead a 'Happy Life'. Ultimately, this is one of the surest path to Peace.